Diane Seed

The Food Lover's Guide to the Gourmet Secrets of

ROME

Universe

Author: Diane Seed
Manager World Travel Guides: Connie Austen-Smith
Managing Editor: Katey Mackenzie
Senior Editor: Isla Love
Senior Designer: Carole Philp
Picture Research: Liz Boyd and Liz Allen
Copy-editor: Hilaire Walden
Proof-readers: Lesley Levene and Ruth Baldwin
Index: Hilary Bird
Cartography: Geoff Chapman
Map Illustration: Chapel Design and Marketing Limited

First published in the United States of America in 2006
by Universe Publishing
A division of Rizzoli International Publications, Inc.
300 Park Avenue South
New York, NY 10010
www.rizzoliusa.com

Originally published in the United Kingdom in 2006
as *Love Food Love Rome* by AA Publishing
A trading name of Automobile Association Developments Limited
Fanum House
Basing View
Basingstoke RG21 4EA
www.theAA.com/travel

The contents of this book are believed correct at the time of printing. Nevertheless, the publishers
cannot be held responsible for any errors or omissions or for changes in the details given in this book
or for the consequences of any reliance on the information provided by the same.
This does not affect your statutory rights.

When following recipes, it is advisable to use all metric, imperial, or cup
measurements and not a mixture.

ISBN-10: 0-7893-1500-9
ISBN-13: 978-0-7893-1500-7

Library of Congress Control Number: 2006925038

2006 2007 2008 2009 / 10 9 8 7 6 5 4 3 2 1

Color separation by MRM Graphics Ltd, Winslow, Buckinghamshire, Great Britain

Printed in China by C & C Offset Printing Co., Ltd

The Food Lover's Guide to the Gourmet Secrets of

ROME

VILLA
BORGHESE

GALLERIA
E MUSEO
BORGHESE

Tevere

Ponte
Margherita

⑧

Mura Aurelle

PALAZZO
BARBERINI

CITTÀ DEL
VATICANA

CAPELLA
SISTINA

CASTEL
SANT'ANGELO

VIA DEL CORSO

VIA SISTINA

④

VIA XX SETTEMBRE

⑤

STAZIONE
TERMINI

BASILICA DI
SAN PIETRO

Ponte
P Sav
Aosta

PANTHEON

PIAZZA
NAVONA

CORSO VITTORIO EMANUELE II

②

FONTANA
DI TREVI

VIA CAVOUR

BASILICA DI
SANTA MARIA
MAGGIORI

①

FORO
ROMANO

VIA CAVOUR

Ponte
Garibaldi

③

TRASTEVERE

COLOSSEO

SAN
CLEMENTE

⑥

SAN GIOVANI
IN LATERANO

VIALE TRASTEVERE

Ponte Sublicio

Tevere

VIALE AVENTINO

Mura Aurelle

FRASCATI

✈

⑨

⑦

↓ SAN PAULO
FUORI LE MURA

Contents

Recipe Contents

Welcome to Rome

When I moved to Rome in 1978 it was not, like many of my English-speaking friends, because I had fallen in love with Rome, deciding that it was the only place on earth I could bear to live. Rather, I had fallen in love with an Italian man, and it was only reluctantly that I moved to Rome. Any city appears more daunting if viewed as a future home, not just a holiday destination. I struggled through the erratic and infuriating muddle that was daily life in Rome in the 1970s, cursing the traffic, the banks, the post office, and the seemingly insurmountable bureaucratic obstacles. When I tried to express my feelings, my Italian was like a rusty sword instead of a rapier, and at home I took to breaking plates as the most effective way of communicating my frustration. I felt I would never belong, I would always be the foreigner.

I don't know when exactly my feelings changed, but I think it was a gradual shift, not a St. Paul on the road to Damascus situation. Rome is a beautiful city but even at the beginning my beloved monuments, the Pantheon and Turtle Fountain, seemed alien. I used to do my food shopping at Testaccio market and it was here that I first thought that, although different, I belonged. The stallholders began to recognize me, and I started to learn new dishes as everyone discussed the best way to prepare cardoons or leeks. My finest moment came when, as I was trying to explain to the butcher that I did not want him to remove the fat from a piece of beef I was planning to roast, he informed the whole shop that "his" *signora inglese* really knew how to choose meat. After this things got easier and I soon fell in love with Rome and Italian cooking. Today for me they are inextricably entwined.

As in the past, all roads lead to Rome, and here we get the best produce from all over Italy. Italian food is regional and people are fiercely loyal to their birthplace. Thirty years ago the trattorias in Rome would have *cucina Emiliana* or *cucina Toscana* written above their door instead of a name, and I remember the excitement when the first Ligurian trattoria opened and started serving pesto. Today boundaries have blurred a little, and people are happy to experiment, but when a Roman talks of *cacio e pepe* or *matriciana* his voice is thick with emotion and it is clear his real love is reserved for Roman dishes. The old proverb says, "*Il pan di casa stufa*" ("Bread from home is boring"), but bread is one thing, pasta and meat another, and the trattorias which serve traditional Roman food are always full.

Rome's market stands and food stores reflect the passing seasons and we go from the myriad shades of green vegetables in spring to the bright colors of summer and the tawny tones of fall. The stallholders shell their peas and fava (broad) beans, trim their green beans and artichokes, and wash their green leafy vegetables. I always end up buying far too much because it all looks so irresistible. When the warm weather arrives the butchers stop selling pork, sausages, and lamb, which are regarded as meat for cold weather, and the fish stands expand as the sea gets more friendly. At this time of year we see the great orange *scorfano*, a vital ingredient for Mediterranean fish soup, large lengths of tuna, and swordfish and glistening piles of shellfish. The local prawns have turquoise eggs, which contrast beautifully with their pink shells.

Italians love to eat, and many visitors to Italy cannot believe the vast quantities of food

they see being consumed at a single sitting. Here there is a proverb that says "The family that eats together stays together", and indeed the main meal of the day is the focal point of family life. Restaurants are usually full of family parties, or groups of friends or businessmen, and the romantic table for two is fairly new to the scene. At this point it is probably helpful to discuss the menu. In Rome the written menu is often misleading, as many daily dishes are decided when the chef sees what looks good in the market. Always ask about the "specials". In restaurants they do not have different sittings, so you won't be asked to leave, even if you have finished your meal, but in a good restaurant you shouldn't occupy a table all evening and only order pasta and salad. Lunch is more relaxed, but each table has to earn its keep.

Antipasto literally means "before the meal" and traditionally this course is made up of stuffed vegetables, prosciutto, salame, olives, and vegetables preserved in olive oil. In summer you get prosciutto e melone and the Caprese of cold mozzarella and tomatoes. The small red cherry tomato from Pachino in Sicily is now an essential part of a Roman dinner, and appears in every course, even on pizza. In restaurants antipasto is usually served to keep you happy while your pasta is being prepared to order, and at home very fresh mozzarella cheese, oozing with milk, is often eaten with a few slices of salame or olives while the water comes to the boil in the pasta pan. Next comes the first course. This usually consists of pasta with fresh vegetables or fish, or a variation of the ubiquitous tomato sauce. It is interesting to note that most families use dry pasta, which goes best with olive oil based sauces. Fresh-egg

pasta — fettuccine — is often served on Sundays or special holidays, but in Italy dry pasta is not regarded as second best. It is served in good restaurants and by fanatically proud home cooks since it belongs to the traditional olive oil based cooking from the south of Italy, where pasta originated. Soups are not very common, although in colder months thick minestre with pulses are offered instead of pasta. The secondo piatto, the main course, usually consists of meat or fish, although some great baked vegetable and cheese dishes can be served as the first or second course. Vegetables or salad are served as a side dish.

Traditionally the meal ends with great bowls of fresh whole fruit in season. First we get cherries, then apricots, nectarines, peaches, plums, and figs. In the fall grapes and persimmons adorn the market stands. In the last few years Rome has discovered berries, known as frutti di bosco, which are served with fresh cream or ice cream. The small wild strawberries from Nemi are traditionally dressed with orange juice. In restaurants desserts used to be rich pastries, but some new light desserts are appearing on the scene, usually "borrowed" from another country, and fresh-fruit ice creams have always been a favorite treat. Then comes caffè. In Italy caffè always means an espresso and

cappuccino is not usually drunk after 11am. For those desiring a less potent brew the caffè is "stained" with milk, macchiato, or you can have it watered down, lungo.

Italian cooking is not complicated or fussy, but you must use good, seasonal ingredients. When making a pasta dish it is important to use good quality durum wheat pasta so that it remains firm when cooked. Italian pasta is exported to most countries and it is usually better than other brands. No sauce, however good, can do anything for a plate of over-cooked pasta. The pasta must be cooked in a large, tall pan, in a great quantity of boiling salted water. If a packet gives directions about the cooking time required, this can only be taken as a rough indication, and you should stand over the pan, testing the pasta at frequent intervals. You shouldn't start to cook the pasta until the sauce is ready, as the sauce waits for the pasta, not the pasta for the sauce. Usually in Rome we do not start to cook the pasta until everyone who has come to eat is ready and waiting. Years ago men would phone as they were leaving work to say "*Butta la pasta*", but this custom has disappeared as Roman traffic has become too unpredictable. It is a mistake to be too lavish with the sauce as the sauce should dress, not drown, the pasta. If you are using Parmesan cheese it should be freshly grated; avoid the temptation

to use packets or drums of ready-grated Parmesan — it is better to substitute a fresh local cheese. In Rome Parmesan is not served with shellfish pasta and I have overheard waiters refusing to bring tourists cheese for spaghetti with clams.

In the past pork lard was used for many traditional Roman dishes, but today this has been replaced by olive oil to make the food lighter and healthier. However, no substitute is accepted when we talk of guanciale. It is believed that the cured cheek of the pig gives inimitable flavor to certain dishes and purists refuse to accept an alternative to the flat, triangular cuts hung up on display in traditional salumerias like Viola in Campo dei Fiori. It has to be sliced by hand and cooked very slowly so that the fat runs out, and it gives a great flavor to the finished dish. Many people have started to substitute pancetta to save time, but I have heard true Romans declare it is not carbonara or Matriciana if it is not made with guanciale.

In the past the Church decreed Tuesdays, Thursdays, and the days before an important religious festival "lean days" and it was not permitted to eat meat. In modern Rome these restrictions no longer exist, but since many Romans prefer fish to meat, they continue to eat fish on these days. Fava beans with Pecorino cheese is the favorite Roman "starter" in spring when the first tender young fava beans appear. On May 1, a national holiday, trucks drive up from the countryside south of Rome and tip out shining heaps of fresh beans to be sold by the side of the main roads leading out of the capital. This is traditionally a day for picnics or eating out, and even on elegant tables the fava beans are served in their pods. Most of the beans are grown in the fertile countryside in the south around Anagni. This area is known as the Ciociara after the comfortable footwear which farmers used to wear, known as *ciocie*. These were square pieces of animal skin, wrapped round the foot and leg, and secured by cords and string wound around the leg. Even today on May 1 some of the country vendors still wear this comfortable, homemade footwear.

The period before Lent is celebrated as Carnevale, which means "farewell meat" in Latin. At Carnevale time Roman bakers sell special sweet pastries and many food stores, such as the butcher Feroci, have trays of *frappe* (fried puff pastry cakes) to offer to their customers. In the Dark Ages sheep grazed in the Forum and Colosseum, and even today on the outskirts of Rome motorists often find their road blocked by a flock of sheep being moved to new pastureland. Young lamb, or the leaner kid, is the meat cooked for special occasions and it is the great dish for Easter, together with torta pasqualina, which is a savory bread usually flavored with cheese or ham and baked with hard-boiled eggs encased in the borders. In Rome there is a dish to celebrate every occasion and whatever the season you will find yourself smiling happily as you sit down to eat.

Campo dei Fiori & Ghetto

The Campo dei Fiori ("field of flowers") takes its name from the time when the piazza was used for grazing cattle. There's no sign of livestock today but the name is still apt, for every morning the square is filled with fruit, vegetable, and flower stands. The neighboring Ghetto dates back to the sixteenth century, when the enforced enclosure of the Jews led to Roman-Jewish dishes such as filetti di baccalà fritti (fried salt cod), which you can still find in the area's Jewish restaurants today.

Campo dei Fiori & Ghetto

Food lovers who visit Rome head straight for the colorful, bustling food market at Campo dei Fiori, where every morning except Sundays and public holidays the piazza is thronged with shoppers carefully checking out the fruit and vegetable stands. Here you'll find fresh local produce piled high, and seasonal specialties such as zucchini (courgette) flowers and Romanesco cauliflowers.

The Campo is dominated by the statue of the gaunt, brooding figure of the philosopher Giordano Bruno, who was burned here for heresy in 1600 by the Inquisition. Before then it had been a smart residential and business area, but after Bruno's death the square became the public execution ground, and the neighborhood went into decline.

Today the grim past is a distant memory. Pigeons perch affectionately on the statue's head and shoulders and people squat on the steps of the plinth, eating just-purchased fruit and irresistible pizza bianca, a plain pizza, with little more than olive oil. During the day the mood is relaxed and light-hearted. In the evening it changes as young revelers take over the square, and the wine bars and restaurants start to fill with discerning and not-so-discerning customers.

The old Jewish Ghetto is at the far end of via dei Giubbonari, which leads off the Campo, and is one of the most historic areas in the city. It was an important site in ancient Rome and the ruins of the Portico d'Ottavia and Teatro di Marcello are still visible. Jews were not treated badly in the classical period, and prisoners of war, brought back as slaves by Pompey the Great when he invaded Judaea, had the possibility of regaining their freedom. Julius Caesar gave them the right to settle anywhere in the Roman Empire and Augustus even organized the grain distribution to avoid the Jewish Sabbath.

With the coming of Christianity the situation changed, and the fortunes of the Jews became dependent on the whims of the different Popes. The Jewish population increased considerably in the sixteenth century, when many Jews fled to Rome from Germany, Spain, and Sicily (which was then still under Spanish rule). By 1555 Pope Paul IV felt numbers were so far out of control that he decreed that all Jews should be forcibly moved to one area. The place chosen was a rather unhealthy and frequently flooded area beside the River Tiber. The Jews were confined in bad sanitary conditions behind three high gates that were locked at sundown and opened in the morning, and so the Ghetto was born. As well as these restrictions on the ability of the Jewish population to move freely, limits were placed on their right to worship and to trade.

The Ghetto endured for more than 300 years and was only finally opened after 1870, when Italy was united. The civil rights that the Jewish population had previously enjoyed were restored, they were allowed to leave the area, and the walls and some of the houses were demolished.

The area near the Portico d'Ottavia and via di Pescaria had been an important fish market that drew Romans from all parts of the city to the area, and the good Jewish cooking also attracted many visitors. Typical dishes from the Ghetto included carciofi alla giudia (whole fried artichokes) and fried fillets of salt cod. Roman cooking owes a great debt to the cuisine of the Ghetto, where traditions remained intact inside the walls. Today, the Ghetto still has its enticing specialty shops and eating places, both kosher and non-kosher, which attract Romans and visitors alike.

Shops in Campo dei Fiori & Ghetto

Mercato di Campo dei Fiori

At the market here, from Monday through Saturday mornings, except public holidays, you'll find the best fruit and vegetables the city has to offer. Most are strictly seasonal, although in the last few years some stands have carried asparagus imported from Peru in the winter months. Some traders make life easier by selling trimmed broccoli, washed spinach, and shucked peas and beans, and labor-intensive artichokes can be bought ready to cook. Claudio, whose table is opposite the flower stands, is known as the Bulgari of fruit and vegetables. He is the only source of dill, rhubarb, and other hard-to-find items, but be aware that it is not only the quality of his produce that wins him the Bulgari title; the prices are correspondingly high. Claudio numbers many of the top restaurants among his customers, and even takes orders by mobile phone. Many of the traders will deliver your shopping, which arrives courtesy of a boy on a suitably Roman motorino.

Andreoli

Time seems to have stood still in this old-style deli. During the winter, sausages and rolled pancetta are made at the back of the store and the prosciutto di montagna, a ham from the mountains with a more robust flavor than either Parma or St. Daniele hams, has been carefully chosen by the owner, who usually slices it off the bone by hand. There is a good selection of cheeses, and the *caciotta* (a semi-soft cheese) and ricotta are produced on the family's farm.

VIA DEI PELLEGRINI 116, 06 6880 2121

Antico Forno del Ghetto

You'll find really good kosher bread in this hundred-year-old bakery. The shop is always busy, and with so many people jostling to be served, a ticket machine for customers to take a number has been installed. However, the crusty bread known as ossi (which means "bones" in Italian), is so good it is well worth the wait. The pizza bianca and pizza rossa (with a tomato based topping) are thin and crisp. A middle-aged man I met there recently said that when he was a pupil at the school nearby they used to take turns to climb out of the window to buy supplies of fresh pizza for the morning break. Next door a young relative, Mauro Urbani, does a brisk trade in non-kosher deli products, and makes panini to order.

PIAZZA COSTAGUTI 30, 06 6880 3012

Antico Forno Roscioli

There is a great choice of bread here including pane integrale (wholewheat bread), loaves containing five cereals, and special breads, such as kosher azzima (unleavened bread), which are baked for Jewish festivals. The pizza bianca is so good that it draws shoppers from all over Rome. Other products include more substantial traditional cakes, such as torta di ricotta (ricotta tart) and the torta della nonna ("grandmother's tart" topped with golden pine nuts). There are also specialties from other regions, such as the Neapolitan pastiere, a cake made with ricotta, wheat grains, candied fruit, and rose water.

Via dei Chiavari 34, 06 6864 045

Attanasio

Emiliano has one of the best fish shops in Rome. When the shutters are opened in the morning, the men are still busy selecting and weighing the fish for the local restaurants and are not ready for customers until after 8.30am. But be sure to get there before 10am to secure the best choice. Try to avoid wearing open sandals or your best shoes because the floor is always swimming in water. It is customary to give a small coin to the man who cleans or fillets your fish. In common with other pescherias, Attanasio is closed on Mondays, and it is also closed on Sundays and in the afternoons.

Via del Biscione 12, 06 6880 1401

Antica Norcineria Viola

Established in 1890 this is one of the few pork stores to survive. The narrow store is festooned with sausages, salami, and prosciutto and the glass counters display every imaginable cut. Viola means "lilac" and distinctive mauve plastic bags used to be standard, but unfortunately the stock ran out and, until they are re-ordered, more quotidian plain white bags have been substituted.

Campo dei Fiori 43, 06 6880 6114

Shops in Campo dei Fiori & Ghetto

Boccione

Three generations of the Limentani family have baked cakes and breads in this pasticceria. Traditional Jewish cakes and bread are geared to the Jewish calendar, and during Pesach (Passover), customers are asked not to bring any yeast products into the store, so as not to contravene the Pesach rules. The rest of the year the delicious cherry and ricotta cakes act as a magnet for sweet-toothed Romans.

Via della Portico d'Ottavia 1, 06 687 8637

Il Fiorentino

Although this shop changed hands in 2005 it has remained a reliably good butcher selling excellent beef, veal, and pork every day except Sunday and Thursday afternoons. As the nearby French Embassy is a customer, salt-marsh lamb is sometimes on sale. An enticing selection of prepared dishes such as *polpette* (meat balls), stuffed zucchini, and various cuts with herbs and vegetables are worth buying.

Campo dei Fiori 17/18, 06 6880 1296

Marcellaio

Giacomo Terracina's kosher butcher is in the heart of the old Ghetto, but the meat and pastrami are of a sufficiently high quality to attract a wide clientele. Three generations of the same family have run the store, and although the premises have changed over the years, it is still very much a family business: while Giacomo takes care of the butchery side of things, Signora Terracina looks after the checkout and their son, Angelo, runs the kosher bistro two doors along the street.

Santa Maria del Pianto 60, 06 686 4659

La Dolce Roma

This famous cake shop is owned by the daughter of the owner of the well-known restaurant Giggetto nearby. This shop is renowned for its Viennese cakes, especially the legendary sachertorte (chocolate layer cake), and the Roman favorite crostata con le visciole (a large tart filled with sour cherry jam) graces the display cabinet. Locals order La Dolce Roma's elaborate cakes for special occasions, while homesick Americans find solace in the brownies and rye bread.

Via della Portico d'Ottavia 20b, 06 689 2196

Roscioli

This is one of Rome's top grocery stores, and is worth the visit just for the amazing range of cheeses, which come from all over Italy, and from other parts of Europe too. If you're interested in sampling "new" products, then this is the place to come. Small tables and chairs are handily placed so you can eat your purchases in the store, accompanied by a glass of wine. Except for the consistent Sunday closing, opening hours are a little erratic and idiosyncratic (it can be irritating to go early to the market only to find that Roscioli is still closed at 8.30am, when most grocery stores have long been open), although it does tend to stay open until quite late in the evening.
Via dei Giubbonari 21, 06 687 5287

Santa Barbara

Seasonal fresh fruit is used in the excellent ice cream sold in this little gelateria, which draws ice cream lovers like a magnet. During the summer, customers sit or stand around chatting and enjoying the refreshing watermelon or berry ice creams. In winter there is less loitering but the delectable citrus fruit varieties still attract customers. Don't head there on Mondays, though, as it's closed.
Largo dei Librari 86, 06 6830 9324

Vito Ruggeri

Established in 1919, this gastronomia used to look very traditional, with great wheels of Parmesan and prosciutto hams hanging behind the counter. Suddenly, almost overnight it seemed, it was given a facelift and the counter was moved to one side instead of being opposite the door. After a slight initial confusion, it was reassuring to discover the same line of white-haired gentlemen waiting to serve and the same good produce. On Fridays there is still a stainless steel bath of traditional soaked salt cod and garbanzo beans (chickpeas) ready for Rome's Friday special, baccalà e ceci (salt cod with garbanzo beans).
Campo dei Fiori 1/2, 06 6880 1091

Il Forno di Campo dei Fiori

There's always a danger that the quality of the wares will slide when a store is enlarged and a key preparation area is removed. Fortunately, that didn't happen at this bakery; the quality is still great and the range has increased. It is *the* place to come for good rye bread and whole wheat breads. The same smiling gentlemen still joke as they "execute" (or cut up) the pizza bianca with murderous slashes, and it is still open Monday through Saturday.
Campo dei Fiori 22, 06 6880 6662

Pages 22–3: Campo dei Fiori is packed with market stands and shoppers in the morning. There is an afternoon lull before the piazza fills up with people heading to the Campo's many wine bars and restaurants.

21

Ditirambo

Lunchtimes are hectic at Ditirambo, with its enviable position near Campo dei Fiori, and when the restaurant opens in the evenings, a babble of English accents fills the room. But as the hours advance, Italian begins to take over and the average age of the clientele drops. The décor is simple, with furnishings leaning toward country chic, the menu varied, and the wine list both comprehensive and fairly priced, with a good choice of half bottles. Roman specialties such as tonnarelli cacio e pepe (pasta with Pecorino cheese and black pepper) are featured on the menu together with specialties from other regions. Vegetables are used in season to make dishes such as the ravioli di zucca (pumpkin ravioli), a dish originally from Mantua, and the restaurant's showcase dish, pasta with zucchini (courgette) flowers.

To follow there is a small choice of vegetarian, fish, and meat dishes. Innovative choices include baked fillet of sea bass with wild fennel and braised vegetables served with a sauce made with spumante, and duck served with marinated red chicory and green apples. In winter, the wild boar with chestnuts is popular. For the sweet toothed, the desserts are irresistible and a bit different than those offered in most Roman restaurants — even the staple tiramisu is made with saffron. Signora Antonia comes in daily to make the desserts, and she is also responsible for the fresh pasta.

PIAZZA DELLA CANCELLERIA 74,
06 687 1626

Giggetto al Portico d'Ottavia

On summer mornings the sidewalk outside the restaurant in the heart of the Ghetto is stacked with crates of artichokes, for this is the temple of the carciofi alla giudia (fried whole artichokes). However, at lunch and dinner from Tuesday through Sunday, there is a menu to satisfy every taste, for the third generation of the Ceccarelli family keeps up the tradition of good food and wine. When the weather is warm, try to get a table outside, from where you can view the majestic ruins of the Portico d'Ottavia built by Augustus. The wine cellar is worth visiting to see the Roman remains.

Via Portico d'Ottavia 21a/22, 06 686 1105

Camponeschi

In the summer you can sit on the terrace of this elegant restaurant in what must be one of the most beautiful squares in Rome and lazily admire the Palazzo Farnese with Michelangelo's work on the upper stories. Top-quality ingredients are used in a large menu of both traditional dishes and some more recent innovations, such as the octopus carpaccio (thinly sliced raw octopus, with an olive oil and vinegar dressing), which is served with puntarelle (asparagus chicory), the Roman vegetable specialty. Next door there is a wine bar where you can enjoy any wine from the list by the glass.

Piazza Farnese 50, 06 687 4927

Il Drappo

Here you'll find a change from the usual dishes on many Roman menus. Il Drappo is a smart, welcoming restaurant near via Giulia, where for over twenty years Romans have been coming to sample the best traditional Sardinian wines and food the city has to offer. The menu pays homage to the beautiful Sardinian coastline with fish dishes such as the delicious series of cold antipasto, spaghetti with sea urchins, and tuna carpaccio. Ossobuco alla drappo (made with sundried tomatoes and sage) and maiolino al profumo di mirto (sucking pig flavored with myrtle) evoke memories of the rugged mountains inland. Owners Walter and Valentina order much of their produce directly from Sardinia, including the traditional (and romantically named) carta di musica, the island's paper-thin crusty bread.

Vicolo del Malpasso 9, 06 687 7365

Minestra di Pasta e Ceci

Pasta and garbanzo bean (chickpea) soup

This thick soup used to be served on days that the Church decreed *magro* (meat-free). Old habits die hard, and today this dish is often eaten on Fridays, or the vigilia, the day before an important religious holiday. This is a very thick minestra and it is not usual to serve grated cheese with it.

SERVES 4

PREPARATION TIME: 20 MINUTES, PLUS OVERNIGHT SOAKING

COOKING TIME: 1 HOUR 30 MINUTES

300g/10oz/1¼ cups garbanzo beans (chickpeas), soaked in water overnight or for 12 hours

1tsp fresh rosemary needles, chopped

4tbsp olive oil

2 garlic cloves, finely chopped

1 dried chile pepper (optional)

120ml/4fl oz/½ cup boiling water

1tbsp tomato purée (optional)

salt and freshly ground black pepper

300g/10oz pasta, preferably fettuccine, broken into short lengths

Drain the garbanzo beans, put into a large saucepan, add 1½ liters/2½ pints/6¼ cups of cold water and the rosemary, cover, and simmer until the beans are very soft. The traditional recipes specify 4 hours, without removing the lid to check, but today's garbanzo beans rarely need more than 1 hour.

Heat the oil in a pan and gently fry the garlic and chile pepper, if using, until the garlic begins to change color. Add the boiling water and tomato purée, if using.

Purée half the garbanzo beans, then stir back into the remaining beans and cooking liquid. Add the garlic mixture and season with salt and pepper to taste. Bring back to the boil and add the pasta.

Cook the pasta for 6–8 minutes, or until soft, and then serve at once. If you are using pasta made without egg it will take a few minutes longer to cook. Make sure you stir the soup from time to time to prevent the pasta sticking to the bottom of the pan.

Spaghetti alla Gricia o Bucatini alla Matriciana

Spaghetti with guanciale and garlic, or bucatini with guanciale, tomatoes, and garlic

This rustic recipe comes from Griciano, in the Sabine hills, but Romans took the dish and made it their own. When a little peeled, chopped tomato is added with the garlic and onion the dish becomes pasta alla Matriciana, after the neighboring town of Amatrice.

SERVES 4

PREPARATION TIME: 15 MINUTES

COOKING TIME: 30 MINUTES

3tbsp olive oil

200g/7oz/⅞ cup guanciale, pancetta, or bacon, sliced

1 small chile pepper

1 small onion, finely chopped

2 garlic cloves, finely chopped

2 ripe tomatoes, peeled and chopped (optional)

salt

500g/1lb 2oz spaghetti or bucatini

100g/3½oz/scant 1 cup freshly grated Pecorino cheese

Gently heat 1 tablespoon of the olive oil, add the guanciale and chile, and let the guanciale fat slowly melt into the oil. Remove and reserve the guanciale. Add the onion, garlic, and tomatoes, if using, to the pan. Cook gently until the onion and garlic are golden brown. Discard the chili, return the guanciale to the pan, and keep warm.

Meanwhile, bring a pan of lightly salted water to the boil. Add the spaghetti or bucatini and cook according to the instructions on the pack until al dente. Drain the pasta and toss with the Pecorino cheese before tossing with the onion and guanciale mixture.

Restaurants in Campo dei Fiori & Ghetto

Piperno

Tourists used to come to eat here when the Ghetto was still a ghetto, locked up at night. Piperno was known as Padre Abram's then and is mentioned in many letters and journals written by foreign visitors. The business was taken over by the Piperno family in 1856 and was run by five generations of the same family until it was bought by the present owners. It is a useful address to know if you are looking for traditional dishes: carciofi alla giudia, pasta e ceci, spaghetti alla carbonara or alla Matriciana. The lamb is reliably good. Book a table in the main room with wall paintings otherwise you will find yourself in the modern "ghetto", a small room full of English-speaking tourists. In the warmer months make the most of the tables outside in the lovely square.

Monte Cenci 9, 06 683 3606

Evangelista

One entrance of this genteel restaurant near the River Tiber is on Lungotevere and the other is on a side street. Inside, Signora Adele presides over the gastronomic kingdom that she inherited from her father. The signature dish is delicious artichokes al mattone (squashed between two bricks and baked) served as an antipasto, a specialty that used to delight the late Pope John Paul II before his rise to eminence restricted his freedom. Several robust soups are served, such as garbanzo bean (chickpea) and chestnut, and it is an excellent place to try vignarola during the short summer period when artichokes, peas, and fava beans are all in season. In the fall and winter, game is usually on offer, and in October and November the sublime scent of white truffles wafts through the restaurant. Geographically, the restaurant is very close to

the Ghetto but the cuisine is Roman, transplanted here many years ago from the Pantheon area, just a few streets away.
VIA DELLE ZOCCOLETTE 11,
06 687 5810

Florida

You can buy pizza by the slice from this world pizza champion pizzeria. One of the "secrets" of their success is to leave the dough to rise slowly for twenty-four hours. They vary the pizza toppings according to the season.
VIA FLORIDA 25, 06 6880 3236

Il Sanpietrino

Oscar, a son of the De Mauro wine family from the Castelli Romani area south of Rome, runs this welcoming, comfortable restaurant set in part of a historic palace just outside the Ghetto. The name is derived from the *sanpietrini*, the traditional cobblestones ladies curse as they try to walk down old Roman streets in heels. There is a sense of occasion to meals here, but the prices are very reasonable and the wine list is great, with wines by the glass, too. The menu has some Ghetto specialties and more innovative dishes such as the turbot with zucchini (courgette) "scales". Among the first courses there is a molded version of pasta alla Norma, which is a pasta dish with tomatoes and eggplant (aubergine), a Sicilian specialty that has become an Italian favorite. The dish was created to celebrate the triumphant début of Vincenzo Bellini's opera of the same name.
PIAZZA COSTAGUTI 15, 06 6880 6471

Hosteria del Pesce

For a theatrical slant to your evening out, come here. The proprietors own fishing boats in Terracina, a small seaside town sixty miles south of Rome, and every morning the best of the night's catch is brought to the capital. It is displayed on a great marble slab at the entrance to the restaurant in all its flamboyant splendor. Flame-colored *scorfani* (scorpion fish) gape open-jawed at the glistening squid, while bowls of mussels and clams crowd next to the oysters flown in that morning from France. There is a great selection of cold and hot antipasti and a top fish dish is the trofie (small pasta twists) with sea bass and lemon. As the evening progresses the choice dwindles, so make sure to get here before 9pm if food is the main attraction. If you prefer to gaze at the would-be celebrities, come later and watch the procession of exotic beauties showing off their unlikely outfits.
VIA MONSERRATO 32, 06 686 5617

Filetti di Baccalà Fritti

Deep-fried salt cod

This is a great Roman specialty. It's a typical antipasto (from the Ghetto area) of fried baccalà fillets served with a deep-fried whole artichoke, and a zucchini (courgette) blossom fried in batter. In Largo dei Librari there is a simple *friggitore* (fry shop) that serves crisp, golden fillets of baccalà. Filettaro a Santa Barbara is only open in the evening, and for a very reasonable price you can enjoy the fried fish with a glass of white wine from the Castelli.

SERVES 4

PREPARATION TIME: 1 HOUR 10 MINUTES, PLUS 24 HOURS SOAKING

COOKING TIME: 15 MINUTES

100g/3½oz/scant 1 cup all-purpose (plain) flour

pinch of salt

725ml/1¼ pints/3 cups water

400g/14oz salt cod, soaked in water for 24 hours

olive oil for deep frying

2 egg whites, beaten until stiff

Sift the flour and salt into a bowl and make a well in the center. Slowly pour in the water, mixing in the flour with a whisk, to make a thick batter. Leave to stand for at least 1 hour.

Meanwhile, drain the fish well and cut into thin strips. Pour enough oil into a pan to cover the fish. Heat the oil until it reaches 180°C/350°F, or when a cube of bread browns in 1 minute.

Fold the egg whites into the batter. Dip the fish into the batter and deep fry in batches for 3–4 minutes, or until crisp and golden brown. Remove the fish from the pan with a slotted spoon, drain briefly on paper towels, and serve at once.

Fiori di Zucca Fritti

Deep-fried zucchini (courgette) flowers in yeast batter

These delicious flowers are usually served in trattorias around the Ghetto with fillets of baccalà and deep-fried whole artichokes. In Rome, pumpkin flowers are used. You can also use the batter with other vegetables cut into batons.

SERVES 4

PREPARATION TIME: 20 MINUTES, PLUS 1½ HOURS FOR THE BATTER TO RISE

COOKING TIME: 10 MINUTES

25g/1oz fresh yeast*

a little tepid water for batter

200g/7oz/1¾ cups all-purpose (plain) flour

12 zucchini (courgette) or pumpkin flowers

125g/4oz mozzarella, cut into 12 batons

4 anchovy fillets, each cut into 3 pieces

oil for deep frying

salt

Crumble the yeast into a little of the tepid water and mix to a smooth cream. Add a little more of the tepid water.

Sift the flour and salt into a bowl, and stir in the yeast liquid. It does not matter if there are a few lumps at this stage; they will disappear as the batter rises. Cover the bowl with a cloth and put in a warm place to rise for 1–1½ hours. When you are ready to use the batter, check its consistency. Add a little more tepid water if it seems too thick but remember that it should cling to the flowers.

Remove the stalks, stamens, and pistils from the zucchini flowers and quickly dip the flowers in water; do not allow them to become waterlogged. Shake dry and wrap in paper towels. Open the flowers carefully and fill each with a baton of mozzarella and a small piece of anchovy fillet.

Heat the oil for deep-frying until it reaches 180°C/350°F, or when a cube of bread browns in 1 minute. Swirl the filled flowers in the batter and carefully drop three or four at a time into the oil. Fry for 1–2 minutes, or until they are golden brown, turning halfway through. Remove with a slotted spoon, drain, and serve at once.

* If fresh yeast is not available, use 1 tablespoon of active dried yeast and stir it into the flour.

The Jewish Influence

When Rome was still part of the Papal States, foreign visitors passed through the forbidding Ghetto gates to eat Jewish delicacies that couldn't be found in the rest of the city. There is an old proverb that says, "*Vesti di turco e mangia da ebreo*" — "Dress like a Turk and eat like a Jew". I understand the compliment to Jewish cooking but I have wild visions of a harem-trousered beauty nibbling a fillet of baccalà or a turbaned Lord Byron lookalike eating artichokes. Today Romans dress in a variety of styles, but even at home, outside the Ghetto, they still enjoy cooking and eating Jewish dishes which originated inside it.

The Jewish community in Rome is the oldest community in Europe. In 161 BC the Maccabees sent envoys to Rome, and merchants soon followed to explore business opportunities. When Rome invaded Judaea some hundred years later, the prisoners of war were brought back as slaves. Some of the present-day Roman Jews are descended from those early slaves. In Christian Rome the fortunes of the Jews changed from Pope to Pope, with the most drastic change occurring after 1492, when Spain expelled any Jews who refused to convert to Christianity. They made their way to Rome, and since Sicily was under Spanish rule at the time, Sicilian Jews came too. The Jewish population almost doubled and Paul IV decided that they must be forced to live together in a controlled area. So, in 1555, the Roman ghetto was created, forty years after the first ghetto, Venice. The Jews were to be confined there for over 300 years.

The Ghetto was cramped and dark and people were forced to build ramshackle upper stories on their houses to provide basic accommodation. In this small space the community became united, sharing good and bad. One of the good things to be shared was food, which often had religious significance. The newcomers, while obeying the same dietary laws as the existing Jews, brought different ways of eating, new vegetables, and new ways of cooking that were soon adopted by all the community. *Friggitori*, or fry shops, were set up in the streets for those people who had no kitchens, and great imagination and ingenuity were used to make ostensibly unpromising ingredients palatable. Many of these dishes remain popular even today.

After Italy was united in 1870, King Victor Emmanuel opened the Ghetto and granted the Jews full citizenship. As they began to mingle with the rest of Rome, and Romans visited the old Ghetto, Jewish cooking slowly began to be discovered. The Jews introduced Rome to their particular way of cooking artichokes, fried whole in deep oil until crisp and golden brown, and to fried fillets of baccalà, and stracciatella, chicken soup with egg and not matzo balls. Rome learned to enjoy eggplant (aubergine) and fennel in new ways, and the interesting addition of raisins and pine nuts comes from the Jews rather than the Arab influence in Sicily, as is often believed.

In the Ghetto, anchovy was used in the same way as non-Jews used pancetta and prosciutto to give a decisive touch of flavor: for example, in the popular filling for zucchini flowers, where it is combined with mozzarella, or in the anchovy dressing that is served with puntarelle (asparagus chicory). Many of Rome's favorite dishes today come from the Ghetto, but most of the people who go there to eat the sublime trio of carciofi alla giudia, fiori di zucca fritti, and fried fillets of salt cod, have no idea of this long history.

Spaghetti alla Carbonara

Spaghetti with creamy egg and guanciale sauce

This very Roman pasta dish is reputed to have been invented by the charcoal-burners who used to spend days in the hills outside Rome, turning the stacked wood piles into charcoal to be used for cooking before gas was piped through the city. The method seems simple but in fact timing is very important to avoid producing pasta with scrambled eggs.

SERVES 4
PREPARATION TIME: 10 MINUTES
COOKING TIME: 10 MINUTES

1tbsp extra virgin olive oil	2tbsp freshly grated Parmesan
150g/5oz/⅔ cup guanciale	1tbsp freshly grated Pecorino
or bacon, diced	cheese
5 eggs	salt and freshly ground
175ml/6fl oz/¾ cup light	black pepper
(single) cream	500g/1lb 2oz spaghetti

Bring a large saucepan of water to the boil for the spaghetti.

Meanwhile, heat the oil and guanciale in a large pan over a low heat until the fat starts to run. This will happen more quickly if you use bacon. Remove from the heat if the fat runs before the spaghetti is ready and then return it to the heat before it is cooked.

Beat the eggs and add the cream. Stir in the grated cheese and a little pepper.

As soon as the water comes to the boil, add salt and then the spaghetti. Cook according to the instructions on the pack until almost al dente.

Drain the pasta and add to the guanciale. Remove the pan from the heat and, working quickly, stir in the egg mixture so that every strand of pasta is coated with a thick yellow cream. Take great care not to let the eggs coagulate. Serve at once with extra black pepper to hand.

Carciofi alla Giudia

Deep-fried whole artichokes

This is the best known dish Rome has inherited from the old Ghetto. Although specialty restaurants seem to serve it nearly all year round, it is best made with very young artichokes, which are available in the late spring and early summer. The central part of the artichoke, the *cimarolo* (bottom or heart), is the part that is usually eaten. The artichokes can be served either hot or when they have cooled to room temperature.

SERVES 4
PREPARATION TIME: 15 MINUTES
COOKING TIME: 20 MINUTES

4 young artichokes	salt and freshly ground
lemon juice	black pepper
olive oil for deep frying	2 lemons, quartered

Remove the coarse outer leaves from the artichokes, and trim and peel the stalk, leaving it 1cm/½ inch long. Rub the cut surfaces of the artichokes with lemon and put in a bowl of lemon juice and water to prevent them discoloring.

When you are ready to cook, heat the oil in a large, deep pan to 150°C/300°F, or until a cube of bread browns in 1–2 minutes.

Meanwhile, drain the artichokes thoroughly and place them head down on a hard surface, pressing firmly so that the leaves open out like a flower. Season them inside. Deep-fry in batches in the hot oil for 10 minutes, keeping them submerged with the back of a slotted spoon. Do not let the oil get too hot at this stage, otherwise the artichokes will not cook evenly. After 10 minutes, increase the heat so the oil temperature reaches 180°C/350°F and continue to cook until the artichokes turn golden brown.

Remove the artichokes from the oil with a slotted spoon and drain on paper towels. If liked, keep warm while the other artichokes are cooking. Serve with lemon wedges.

Landmarks

This part of Rome is so packed full of history you could explore the narrow, bustling streets forever yet constantly stumble across fresh discoveries, from statues to synagogues, through to palaces and piazzas. Through the labyrinthine narrow streets, republican, imperial, medieval, Renaissance, and papal Rome are each built up, layer upon layer, into the proverbial embarrassment of riches.

Fontana delle Tartarughe

The small "tortoise" fountain (top left), one of the most charming in the city, was built in 1581 by Taddeo Landini for the Mattei family for "their" square, piazza Mattei. Four graceful young men, cast in bronze, rest their feet on the heads of dolphins, as they each hold up a wriggling tortoise to drink from the fountain. In fact, the tortoises were only added about a hundred years after the fountain was erected.

Palazzo della Cancelleria

Built in 1485, the Cancelleria was funded by Cardinal Raffaele Riario's winnings from gambling and he used the building for Church administration. Architect and painter Giorgio Vasari is said to have boasted that he designed and finished one of the large rooms in just one hundred days, and, reputedly, a critical Michelangelo said he could well believe it.

Palazzo Farnese

Just a stone's throw from the Campo dei Fiori, the beautiful Renaissance Palazzo Farnese (left), the French Embassy since 1871, occupies one side of elegant piazza Farnese. The palace was built for Cardinal Alessandro Farnese, who later became Pope Paul III. The top floor was designed by Michelangelo. In the fountain in the center of the piazza, stone lilies, the emblem of the Farnese family, splash water into a huge granite bath that was "borrowed" from the Terme di Caracalla.

Pompey the Great's Theater

Perhaps the most important and certainly the largest landmark, Pompey the Great's theater, can only be glimpsed as ruins underground, or imagined. Via Grotta Pinta curves in a semicircle as it follows the line of the great amphitheater, and in piazza Biscione and piazza Paradiso there are restaurants where you can eat among the ruins. The theater was huge, with a colonnade stretching from via Chiavari up to largo Argentina.

In Shakespeare's *Julius Caesar*, Caesar is murdered in the Capitol at the base of Pompey's statue, "which all the while ran blood". In fact, the murder took place in the theater beside the statue in the colonnade and the spot where Caesar probably fell is on the entrance steps to the present day Teatro Argentina. It is said that, despite his twenty-three stab wounds, he wrapped his toga around him as he fell, to maintain his dignity. At the time of Caesar's death Cleopatra was living in Rome at his villa across the River Tiber along with his wife, Calpurnia.

Portico d'Ottavia & Teatro di Marcello

In the Ghetto itself the Portico d'Ottavia and the Teatro di Marcello are the most important Roman ruins. The Portico was named by Augustus in honor of his sister Ottavia, who was the wife of Mark Antony. It was part of a large complex, the Circus Flaminius, where there had been great temples to Jupiter and Juno. Augustus restored the building in AD 32, and the neighboring Teatro di Marcello was named after Ottavia's son, Marcellus, who was married to Augustus's daughter, Julia. In the Middle Ages the Portico took on a more functional role when it became the site of the city's fish market.

The name of the nearby church of Sant'Angelo in Pescheria recalls the fish market. This is one of the Christian churches where the Jews of the Ghetto were forced to listen to Christian sermons.

Sinagoga

In 1904, a huge synagogue was built overlooking the Tiber and its great dome is still visible from all over the city. Today the synagogue houses the Jewish museum, and despite the unhappy associations, this area is still a meeting place for the Roman-Jewish community, with narrow streets packed with Jewish restaurants and kosher grocery stores.

Pantheon & Piazza Navona

In the historic heart of Rome, bounded by the River Tevere to the west and via del Corso to the east, ancient buildings, elegant piazzas, and churches protecting their treasure of Caravaggios hide themselves in the maze of narrow streets and lanes. Romans and visitors alike feel it is a privilege to dine in such a beautiful setting and consequently the area is overflowing with places to eat. Traditional family-run trattorias, top seafood restaurants, and two of the most famous (and best) coffee bars in Rome all jostle for space in this hub of Roman life.

Pantheon &
Piazza Navona

Here in the historic center the classical age and the Renaissance go hand in hand. There are numerous palaces from the great families who became great because they had a Pope or at least an influential cardinal to feather the family nest. A few, like the Massimo family, claim important Romans as their ancestors. Every building deserves a pause to read the historic information displayed outside.

One of Rome's top tourist attractions is the Pantheon, a 2,000-year-old place of worship, whose graceful portico dominates piazza della Rotonda. Romans and visitors alike flock to nearby piazza Navona to see the three magnificent sculptural fountains, or more likely than not, just to enjoy the fun atmosphere and relax with an ice cream.

Further east, Palazzo Doria Pamphilj in via del Plebiscito, is one of the largest palaces in Rome, and home to one of the city's most prestigious art collections. There are four picture galleries containing a collection of paintings from the sixteenth to eighteenth centuries and sculptures commissioned by the Pamphilj Pope Innocent X, including a portrait of the Pope in gallery three which was painted by Diego Velasquez.

Not far away, piazza Venezia, with the white, theatrical Monumento a Vittorio Emanuele II (the first king of a united Italy), is right at the center of Rome. The nearby Palazzo Venezia was started in 1455 by the Venetian Pietro Barbo when he became a cardinal, and was then enlarged when he become Pope Paul II in 1464. The Popes continued to live in a wing up until the sixteenth century.

In the nineteenth century Napoleon made the Palazzo Venezia the seat of the French government, and between 1930 and 1944

Mussolini set up his government there, using the balcony for making his speeches haranguing the people. Nowadays, many official events with visiting foreign dignitaries are held in the Palazzo during the year. The traffic in the piazza can be chaotic.

There must be more places to eat in this area than in any other part of Rome, but as there are not many residents the shops do not offer the variety found elsewhere. There is a small market in piazza delle Coppelle and the famous historic butcher Angelo Feroci. Gelaterie (ice cream parlors) are plentiful, and on hot summer evenings residents complain that it is impossible to find parking until after 3am as all of Rome comes to round off the evening with an ice cream. At lunchtime the grocery stores make up panini to order and the takeout pizza shop in via Pie di Marmo does a roaring trade with pupils from the nearby high school. Around the Pantheon, many of the restaurants cater to politicians from the Italian parliament. Near the Senate House there are more pricey eating places for politicians, but the once-famous restaurants around piazza Navona have become more orientated to inexpensive tourism.

Shops in Pantheon & Piazza Navona

Ai Monasteri

All the items on sale, ranging from jellies (jams), liqueurs, chocolate, medicinal tinctures, and beauty aids, have been made in Italian monasteries by monks. Much of what the monks produce is made according to centuries-old recipes.

Corso Rinascimento 72, 06 6880 2783

Angelo Feroci

The shop dates back to the 1890s and every day except Sunday, though not on Thursday or Saturday afternoons, there is a great selection of meat displayed on the original marble counters. In another display case there are ready-prepared meat dishes and even cooked vegetables like carciofi alla giudia. The skilled young men behind the counter look like modern-day pirates with their colorful headscarves and long knives, but they deal patiently with their sometimes demanding customers and soothe even the most querulous signora. At Christmas, Easter, and other festivals they prepare gastronomic feasts to order.

Via della Maddalena 15, 06 6830 7030

L'Antica Erboristeria Romana

This fascinating shop dates back to the nineteenth century and it still has many of the original fittings. I come here to buy my kitchen supply of saffron and fennel seeds and enjoy gazing at the pots and potions and inhaling the exotic scents in the air.

Via Torre Argentina 15, 06 687 9495

La Corte

This minute shop which sells wonderful smoked salmon was started by an Englishman in the early 1970s, and at that time he did his own smoking in the Sabine hills outside Rome, near the villa of the Roman poet Horace. He introduced Rome to the taste of smoked salmon and it proved so popular that today it is available in most supermarkets and salumerias. However, La Corte is still the best, and the delectable wild Canadian salmon attracts connoisseurs. They also sell other smoked fish, caviar, and bottarga (pressed dried tuna or mullet roe).

Via della Gatta 1, 06 678 3842

La Deliziosa

This very small traditional cake store is tucked away in a narrow alley off Corso Vittorio Emanuele. It is famous above all for the torta di ricotta (ricotta tart or cheesecake), but you'll also find old favorites like apple charlottes and lemon tart as well as delicious mimose, which are a type of coconut cake colored yellow and named after the pretty yellow flower.

VICOLO SAVELLI 50, 06 6880 3155

Despar

It might seem strange to include a supermarket in this selection, but this shop has gradually earned a place in Italian food guides for its wonderful cheese counter. There are cheeses from most Italian regions, and in an area with more eating places than food shops it is a useful place to know.

VIA GIUSTINIANI 18B, 06 683 3166

Dolciumi e Frutta Secca

In this small shop Patrizia Onorati sells all the dried fruits and nuts needed for baking, plus baking chocolate, and gelatin sheets for pannacotta. It is an essential address for the home cook.

CORSO RINASCIMENTO 8, 06 686 5268

Giolitti

At the end of the nineteenth century via del Corso had many elegant bars around the Galleria, and Giolitti formed part of that tradition. Most of the other bars have disappeared or changed out of all recognition, but Giolitti continues to be an essential Roman attraction. The magnet that attracts the constant stream of clients that swells to a river in the summer months is the ice cream. Here you will find over fifty different flavors, including pistachio, chocolate liqueur, and Zabaglione. There are various sizes of cones and coppette (little tubs) that you can take out or you can eat sitting down in the large, airy, comfortable rooms and enjoy your ice cream in style.

VIA UFFICIO DEL VICARIO 40, 06 699 1243

Sant'Eustachio

Here you are in the temple of great coffee and the worshippers are prepared to stand in line and be squashed together in order to enjoy the divine aroma and their two or three sacred sips of rich coffee. It's always crowded here in this beautiful coffee bar which has mosaic floors and original furniture, and at peak times it is difficult even to get near the bar. To the uninitiated it can just seem like a scrum, but the first taste brings about instant conversion.

Sant'Eustachio has been producing coffee here for nearly fifty years and their secret is that they roast the beans on the premises, at the back of the store. You can enjoy a caffè or morning cappuccino or purchase the roasted beans to take away, wrapped in Sant'Eustachio's signature yellow packaging, which has a stag's head as its emblem. As an indication of how strongly Romans feel about their historic coffee shop, they argue about the rival merits of Sant'Eustachio and Tazza d'Oro with almost, but not quite, the same passion as they debate the merits of Rome's rival soccer teams Roma and Lazio.

PIAZZA SANT'EUSTACHIO 82, 06 6880 2048

Forno

This is a very old-fashioned panetteria (bakery) with courteous service; even at the end of the working day the assistants still have the time and energy to joke with their customers. Traditional crusty loaves and pizza bianca, and the selection of time-honored cookies and cakes are the reasons to come here, but try to avoid lunchtimes when the shop is packed.

VIA DEI PASTINI 126, 06 679 4148

Fratelli Carilli

In the past pork butchers were very common in Rome, but nowadays it is rare to find one that specializes in fresh pork and pork products, as most butchers tend to sell all kinds of meat. Here there is also a salumeria section with a wide choice and they also stock other traditional ingredients like pulses, dried pasta, and cheese. On Fridays there are tanks of soaked baccalà (salt cod) and garbanzo beans (chickpeas) on display. The three brothers who own the shop tend to bicker among themselves, although they sell a superb mozzarella di bufala (buffalo mozzarella), so when this is on your shopping list it is worth ignoring the dark mutterings.

VIA TORRE ARGENTINA 11, 06 6880 378

Moriondo e Gariglio

This historic shop makes delicious home-made chocolates in the Piemonte tradition to delight every taste. Before all important festivities the shop is thronged with people ordering chocolates, jellied fruits, and marrons glacés which are finished off while you wait. My favorites are the slivers of orange and lemon peel covered with dark, bittersweet chocolate.

VIA PIÈ DI MARMO 21, 06 699 0856

Tazza d'Oro

In Rome, roasting coffee beans is not something that you can just decide to do and then open a bar — you need a special license. Tazzo d'Oro is the only place in the center of Rome that has one. The shop is always busy, with people coming to enjoy an excellent coffee and buy coffee beans to take home. The beans can be ground on request and the delicious aroma pervades the shop as people shout at each other to be heard over the noise of the grinder.

VIA DEGLI ORFANI 84, 06 6789 792

Restaurants in Pantheon & Piazza Navona

Alceste al Buon Gusto

In the past you had to drive to the town of Anzio to enjoy the Regolanti family's excellent fish dishes. Now that the family has opened this branch right by the Senate, you can dine on the freshest fish, oysters, and prawns at very fair prices, considering that fresh fish is never cheap, and there is an excellent wine list. CORSO RINASCIMENTO 70, 06 686 1312

L'Altro Mastai

This has quickly become one of Rome's top restaurants for dinner, Tuesday through Saturday. The elegant dining room enjoys masterly lighting and there is a comfortable space between the tables. The creative menu reveals Fabio Baldassare's experiences in other European cities. In the fall, dishes include veal fillet with black truffles. There is also a wine bar for those who just want a quick drink. VIA G. GIRAUD (CORNER VIA DEI BANCHI NUOVI), 06 6830 1296

Baffetto

This well-loved Roman pizzeria has been producing thin, crisp pizza in the evenings for over forty years. It's always crowded here and you may well have to wait to get a table. Italian speakers might wonder why a restaurant should be called *baffetto* ("mustache"), but sight of the owner's face quickly makes everything clear: he wears a luxurious mustache. VIA DEL GOVERNO VECCHIO 114, 06 686 1617

Da Armando al Pantheon

For over forty years the Gargioli family has had a reputation for providing their faithful following with reliable, unpretentious food. Typical Roman dishes like pasta e ceci (pasta with garbanzo beans) or coda alla vaccinara (oxtail stew) are interspersed with some innovations like duck with prunes. There is a modest choice of wines with decent half bottles. Booking for dinner is essential, although the restaurant is closed on Saturday evenings, as well as all day Sunday.

Salita de'Crescenzi 31, 06 6880 3034

Enoteca Corsi

This is a family-run Rome institution from another era. Every lunchtime (except Sunday) the long tables are thronged with local workers, canny visitors, and hungry residents. A blackboard in the window shows the daily menu, which usually consists of three first courses and main dishes, with a vegetarian alternative, and a couple of desserts. The menu is made up of traditional home cooking with hearty, filling dishes such as bean soup, gnocchi, and roasted codfish served with garlic and potatoes.

Via del Gesù 87/88, 06 6790 0821

Fortunato al Pantheon

Politicians of many persuasions come here, as can be seen from the photographs on display in the entrance. The menu is classical Italian and the service is friendly but professional. Every day (except Sunday) there is a list of the chef's suggestions plus the general menu which offers a choice of classic dishes like spaghetti alle vongole (with clams), polpette (small meat balls) with artichokes, and melanzane alla Parmigiana (eggplant baked in tomato sauce, with Parmesan). In season there is delicious tagliolini with white truffles. The desserts include a good crema caramella and majestic jelly-filled tarts known as crostate. Unusually for Rome, there is even a special menu for celiacs and diabetics.

Via del Pantheon 53, 06 679 2788

Pomodori al Riso

Tomatoes stuffed with rice

In the summer months Rome's markets sell great round red tomatoes, labeled "di riso" that are used just for this favorite dish.

SERVES 4

PREPARATION TIME: 20 MINUTES, PLUS COOLING TIME

COOKING TIME: 50 MINUTES

2tbsp extra virgin olive oil, plus extra for oiling

8 large, firm, ripe tomatoes

8tbsp carnaroli rice

2 garlic cloves, finely chopped

8 fresh basil leaves, roughly torn into pieces

1tbsp chopped fresh parsley

salt and freshly ground black pepper

Preheat the oven to 180°C/350°F/gas mark 4. Lightly oil a baking dish, making sure that it is large enough to hold the tomatoes.

Carefully slice the tops off the tomatoes and keep to one side to act as lids. Scoop out the centers of the tomatoes, without piercing the skin, and sieve the pulp to remove the seeds. Mix the sieved pulp with the remaining ingredients, except the oil. Half fill the tomatoes with this mixture and then replace the lids.

Arrange the tomatoes standing upright in the baking dish and drizzle the oil over the top. Bake for about 50 minutes, or until the tomatoes are soft and the rice is cooked. Then leave at room temperature for at least 20 minutes before serving. Serve from the baking dish.

Filetti di Rombo al Cartoccio

Turbot fillets baked in paper

In Rome, turbot (*rombo*) is one of the most prized fish. When presented with a superb *rombo*, the Roman emperor Domitian called a council meeting to decide how to cook it, and ordered a special plate to be made on which to display the prized specimen. This method of cooking the fish fillets while wrapped in baking parchment, allows them to absorb the flavors of the garlic and parsley without losing their moisture. The result is a delicately flavored, tender fish.

SERVES 4

PREPARATION TIME: 20 MINUTES

COOKING TIME: 20 MINUTES

4 turbot fillets, each about the size of your hand

salt and freshly ground black pepper

1 garlic clove, finely chopped

2tbsp chopped fresh parsley

200g/7oz/⅞ cup butter

4 young scallions (spring onions), finely chopped

1 dried chile pepper, crushed

grated zest of 1 lemon

Preheat the oven to 180°C/350°F/gas mark 4. Cut four squares of baking parchment. Season the fish fillets, sprinkle on the garlic and parsley, and then roll them up tightly. Place each fillet near one side of a square of baking parchment. Fold in the sides of the parchment, then roll up into a package and tie in place with thin kitchen string.

Arrange the packages in a single layer in a shallow baking dish and cook in the oven for 15 minutes.

Just before the fish is ready, gently heat the butter in a pan along with the scallions, chile pepper, and lemon zest. Do not let the butter brown. The idea is simply to release the flavors into the butter. This should take about 5 minutes.

Remove the fish from the oven, discard the string and paper, and serve drizzled with the butter sauce.

Myosotis

The ingredients for the dishes served in this warm, lively, welcoming restaurant very near the Pantheon are chosen with care. The family produces its own olive oil, and the father, Gabriele, who is a butcher by trade, selects first-class meat. The antipasto of focaccia, ricotta, and a selection of salami is always popular, while the fresh pasta dishes are considered to be some of the best around. Delicious fish dishes include baked swordfish stuffed with capers and breadcrumbs, simple grilled prawns, and calamari. The extensive wine list has some of the best prices in Rome. VICOLO DELLA VACCARELLA 3/5, 06 686 5554

Quinzi e Gabriele

The rich, the famous, and the beautiful flock to this smart, fashionable fish restaurant, which is considered by many to be the top fish restaurant in Rome, with prices to match. Select from oysters which are flown in daily from France, carpaccio di pesce ai sapori mediterranei, spaghetti all'aragosta (with lobster), and scorfano all'acqua pazza (scorpion fish cooked in seawater). There is a small courtyard where you can dine outside on balmy summer evenings. PIAZZA DELLE COPPELLE 6, 06 687 9389

Pizzeria la Montecarlo

Good, thin, crisp pizzas are available here at lunchtimes, as well as in the evenings, except on Mondays which is all-day closing. Their signature pizza montecarlo has tomato, mozzarella, mushrooms, artichokes, sausage, eggs, peppers, onion, and olives. In the evenings the place is jolly but crowded, so you are discouraged from lingering on after you have finished your meal! With this in mind, it is a better place for a pre- or post-movie pizza, than for a long discussion or a romantic night out. VICOLO DEI SAVELLI 12/13, 06 686 1877

Romilo

The elegant dining room with minimalist décor attracts both politicians and businessmen, and there are some smaller rooms for private dining and discreet discussions. The menu provides an interesting combination of traditional Roman and more innovative dishes. The gnocchi are very good, as is the paccheri (large pasta tubes with red mullet), and there is a vegetable terrine for those who don't eat meat or fish.

VIA DI CAMPO MARZO 13, 06 689 3499

Trattoria

This fashionable, modern restaurant on two floors is a refreshing alternative to the many trattorias and restaurants which serve only traditional Roman cooking. The menu here is based on Sicilian dishes interpreted in a light, creative, and imaginative way. Expect such delights as pasta alla Norma, caponata (a type of ratatouille), and that most Sicilian of desserts, cassata. You can watch your dinner being prepared in the kitchen while sitting at your table.

VIA DEL POZZO DELLE CORNACCHIE 25, 06 6830 1427

Vecchia Locanda

Housed in a fifteenth-century building, this is a lovely setting in which to enjoy Roman dishes cooked with the freshest of ingredients. For first course the tonnarelli are served with different sauces and the fresh ravioli are excellent. Other delicious dishes include pasta alla carbonara, spaghetti alla Matriciana, and pasta with asparagus, clams, and shrimp.

VICOLO SINIBALDI 6, 06 6880 2831

Tagliolini al Salmone

Tagliolini with smoked salmon sauce

Smoked salmon and cream produce an opulent, quickly prepared sauce that always makes this seem a special occasion dish.

SERVES 4
PREPARATION TIME: 10 MINUTES
COOKING TIME: 10 MINUTES

150g/5oz smoked salmon	500g/1lb 2oz tagliolini
25g/1oz/2tbsp butter	salt and freshly ground
1 small onion, finely chopped	black pepper
250ml/9fl oz/scant 1¼ cups light (single) cream	

Cut half the salmon into thin strips and roughly chop the rest. Melt the butter in a saucepan set over a low heat, add the onion, and cook gently until it softens; do not allow it to brown. Add the roughly chopped salmon and the cream and warm through gently before pouring into a blender or food processor and mixing to a smooth sauce. Pour into a pan large enough to contain the cooked pasta. Put the pan over a low heat about 5 minutes before the pasta is ready.

Cook the pasta in a large pan of lightly salted boiling water, according to the instructions on the pack, until al dente. Drain and toss with the salmon cream sauce and stir in the ribbons of smoked salmon, lifting and separating the strands. Season with freshly ground black pepper and serve at once.

Spaghetti ai Carciofi

Spaghetti with artichokes

Romans love artichokes and they appear in many guises. This is one of my favorites — spaghetti dressed with artichokes cooked in olive oil with garlic and peperoncino (dried chile pepper). I buy fresh chiles every July and August and thread them on to strings, which then hang in my kitchen for the rest of the year. As they dry out, so their flavor in this dish improves. When artichokes are in season I cook this dish at least twice a week.

SERVES 4
PREPARATION TIME: 20 MINUTES
COOKING TIME: 20 MINUTES

6 artichokes	1 dried chile pepper
2 lemons	salt
4tbsp extra virgin olive oil	2tbsp boiling water
2 garlic cloves, finely chopped	500g/1lb 2oz spaghetti

Remove the outer leaves from the artichokes and, using a sharp knife, cut off the tough tips from the remaining leaves. Cut the artichokes into quarters. Rub the cut surfaces with half a lemon. Squeeze the remaining lemon juice into a bowl large enough to hold the artichokes and top up to halfway with water. Remove and discard the hairy "choke" at the center of each artichoke and cut each segment into thin slices. Drop the slices into the bowl as soon as you finish cutting them.

Heat the oil, garlic, and chile in a large skillet for a few minutes. Drain, rinse, and dry the artichoke slices and add to the oil. Cook gently, stirring for a few minutes before adding a little salt and the boiling water. Cover and simmer for 10 minutes.

Meanwhile, cook the pasta in lightly salted boiling water, according to the instructions on the pack, until al dente. Drain, reserving about a cupful of the cooking water. Toss the spaghetti with the artichoke mixture. If the pasta seems too dry, add a large spoonful of the reserved pasta cooking water. Serve at once.

Il Convivio di Troiani

Over the years restaurants change as the chef moves on or the owner gets tired. What a pleasure to find that after sixteen years Il Convivio is still my favorite elegant restaurant in Rome. The brothers of the Troiani family have matured but they are still full of enthusiasm, and the welcome is always warm and spontaneous. The menu is imaginative without striving for improbable combinations for the sake of innovation, and I discover new wine treasures with every visit. The best part of all is that the restaurant has remained natural and relaxed without any hype.

This story begins like a fairy tale: "Once upon a time there were three brothers who decided to come to Rome to seek their fortune…" The Troiani brothers, Massimo, Giuseppe, and Angelo, were brought up in Ascoli Piceno in the Le Marche region of Italy. Massimo and Giuseppe worked in a bar in Riccione, on the Adriatic coast, occasionally taking the younger Angelo to help them. Angelo liked the atmosphere and showed an aptitude for the work, so he was sent to a *scuola albergiere* (restaurant school).

In 1987 the three brothers came to Rome to look for somewhere they could work together. It proved difficult and a little daunting and they were about to give up when they found a hotel restaurant they could take over. They ran this successfully for a year until they decided they were ready to start their own restaurant. Their first Il Convivio opened in 1990, when the brothers were in their twenties. They had great success and soon the restaurant was ranked third in Rome. By 1999 they needed more space, so they took over 300 square meters of an old elevator factory near piazza Navona in the heart of the city. This is the elegant but warmly welcoming present-day Il Convivio. With the help of talent, passion, and a lot of hard work they have achieved a happy ending.

Massimo, the eldest, is in charge of the wines. His enthusiasm is infectious and choosing your wine becomes a voyage of discovery. Il Convivio has an outstanding wine list and an equally exciting list of unusual spirits. The second brother, Giuseppe, has the unobtrusive charm of a top manager and things run very smoothly in his hands. He anticipates any potential problem and irons out any wrinkles before they have time to develop. In the kitchen there is a brigade of twelve and head chef Angelo inspires them all. His greatest asset is an ability to combine familiar ingredients in an innovative way, something which can't be taught at restaurant school. He sources most of the produce locally and personally selects all his top-quality *materie prime* (raw ingredients). When the brothers started working in Rome, Angelo ordered fish from the same shop as most good restaurants, but now he orders the fish and seafood to be brought straight from the fishing boats to the restaurant. His herbs and vegetables come from Claudio, a trader in the Campo dei Fiori market, who enjoys seeking out unusual produce.

An elderly lady used to come in every morning to make the pasta, with her long rolling pin tucked firmly under her arm, but now two young men are in charge of what is the cornerstone of any Italian restaurant. Women have taken over many of men's traditional roles, but here the process has been reversed.

The menu changes constantly and it is best to go without any firm idea of what you want to eat. You will find a tempting list of fish, poultry, and meat and part of the enjoyment is the glorious indecision. There are always some Roman favorites given a new twist, such as pasta alla carbonara with zucchini (courgettes). There is a tasting menu but I like to agonize over the menu, choose, change my mind, choose again, and then finally talk about the wine with Massimo.

VICOLO DEI SOLDATI 31, 06 686 9432

OPEN EVENINGS ONLY, MONDAY THROUGH SATURDAY

Landmarks

One of the charms of Rome is the unexpected. Other capital cities seem to announce their great buildings well in advance by wide approach roads and minor edifices, but Rome can catch you by surprise. At night, walking down one of the old, dimly lit, narrow streets, you turn a corner and are confronted by the calm, splendid portico of the Pantheon, with its great Corinthian columns and inscribed pediment.

Fontana dei Fiumi

The most eye-catching feature of piazza Navona is Gianlorenzo Bernini's famous Fountain of the Four Rivers (below right). It shows the main rivers of the four continents: the Danube in Europe, the Ganges in Asia, the Nile in Africa, and the Plate River in the New World (as it was then). It is popularly believed that Bernini's rival Borromini built the Church of Sant'Agnese in Agone in front of the fountain, and that the statue representing the Nile covers his face as if to shield his eyes from Borromini's work. However, the story is apocryphal as the fountain predates the church. The true story is that the face of the Nile is covered because its source was still unknown at that time.

Pantheon

The Pantheon is one of Rome's most arresting sights. The original was built in 27 BC by Marcus Agrippa, Augustus's general and son-in-law, whose name is still clearly visible in the inscription, which translates as: "Marcus Agrippa, son of Lucius, third time Consul, built this." In fact, the words are misleading, as the building as it is today was built nearly one hundred years after his death, by Hadrian, using some of the original stones. The Pantheon has survived with its majesty intact although it has been plundered and vandalized over the ages. The wall veneers of precious stones were stolen, and the gilded roof tiles were stripped off and then lost in a shipwreck on their way to Byzantium. It was only when the Popes returned from exile that the Pantheon was cleaned and its dignity restored.

Today tourists gaze up at the oculus (left), the hole in the roof, which is the only source of natural light in the building and where water pours in on a rainy day. The church is a mausoleum for members of Italy's royal family and is also the final resting place of Renaissance artist Raphael.

Until 1847 a fish market was held by the Pantheon in piazza della Rotonda around the lovely Renaissance fountain and Ramses II obelisk. You can still see the holes that were made in the portico columns for the poles that supported awnings for the market stands.

Piazza della Minerva

As well as the church, this piazza is home to Bernini's little elephant statue with its small obelisk that was found nearby (right). The elephant has a large saddlecloth because the people who commissioned the statue doubted the weight-bearing capacity of the sculpture due to the space between the elephant's legs.

Piazza Navona

The piazza started life as the stadium of Domitian, and was built for athletic games. Its name, Circus Agonalis, became corrupted to n'Agona and eventually Navona. The piazza is an elongated oval and follows the shape and size of the original stadium. It survived the

Pages 58–9: the Fontana del Nettuno is one of three magnificent fountains in piazza Navona, and depicts Neptune, the god of the sea, battling with a sea monster.

centuries and has been used for many different spectacles. In 1485 the central area was paved, but the tiered seats remained until they gradually gave way to eating places and inns. Their foundations can be glimpsed in some surrounding cellars.

Today piazza Navona is still a place for pleasure. At Christmas, little stands sell toys, balloons, and festive decorations, and an army of Father Christmases prowls in search of prey. Throughout the year artists solicit custom for their lightning quick portraits and out-of-work young people, wrapping themselves in gold lamé, stand motionless as embalmed pharaohs. The bars have outside heaters to warm their customers who come here for a coffee or an aperitivo.

Trastevere

This *quartiere* of Rome has always
felt a little different. Its position
on the other side of the River Tiber
has given it a "village" feel you
don't find in other parts of the city.
In the imperial age the land here
was given over to vineyards and
farms; now it is a place where
people come to meet and spend
their evenings in the area's many
bars, restaurants, and pizzerias.
Growing tourism has affected
the prices and quality in some
of Trastevere's restaurants, but
despite that, to miss out on dinner
on a warm summer evening here
would be to miss out on one of
Rome's great experiences.

Trastevere

Trastevere, across the River Tiber (or Tevere in Italian), used to be a working-class area and the people who lived here were proud of being "different". They claimed to be the only citizens descended from the ancient Romans, and their July celebration "Festa del Noantri" (feast of we others) was full of gaiety and warmth. Artisan workshops and stables for the *carrozzella* (carriage) horses lined the narrow, winding streets, which were named after the different trades and their products, like "straw" and "baskets", and lines of washing stretched across the alleyways. At the end of the week, Romans from other areas flocked to Trastevere to enjoy the bohemian, hedonistic lifestyle, and the great central piazza of Santa Maria was the hub of what seemed a perpetual street party. Food was good everywhere and trattorias were chosen by mood and whim not by restaurant guide.

Today, things have changed. Wealthy Italians and foreigners have bought up what were once humble apartments and fashionable boutiques have replaced the workshops, although the native dialect of Rome is still spoken by some of the area's traditional inhabitants, the Trasteverini.

Trastevere at night has become the mecca of the young. To eat well you must choose wisely, not forgetting to check the prices, and book in advance. During the week Trastevere is still very beautiful and you can stroll around the cobbled *vicoletti* (alleys) and *piazzette* (small squares), admiring the faded terracotta-colored walls and quaint houses. The ideal way to see Trastevere at its best is to spend a weekday morning exploring the churches, specialty shops, and San Cosimato market, before enjoying an aperitivo before lunch.

In Trastevere you'll find that most of the eating places are trattorias. As many of them cater solely to the tourist trade it is possible to eat badly here. However certain dishes are so much a part of Trastevere lore it is difficult to go wrong if you see them on the menu. If you order cacio e pepe together with a carafe of house red wine, you can sit back and enjoy. Cacio e pepe is usually made with a long pasta, tonnarelli, and it is simplicity itself. It is the ultimate comfort food and is made with the pungent sheep's cheese known as Pecorino and freshly ground black pepper which adds a "bite". *Cacio* is an old Roman word for cheese and here the cheese is always Pecorino. If you have a kitchen and wish to duplicate the experience at home, make sure you buy good quality mature Pecorino. The wonderful cheese store Antica Caciara on via San Francesco a Ripa has a great selection of cheeses and connoisseurs usually buy their Pecorino here.

Trastevere could be compared to a modern day Janus. One face is turned toward the narrow picturesque streets, the other toward two beautiful Renaissance palaces. Palazzo Corsini, which now houses part of the Galleria Nazionale d'Arte Antica, is full of priceless works of art by masters such as Rubens and Caravaggio, while just across via della Lungara is the sixteenth-century Villa Farnesina, dreaming in its beautiful gardens.

One of the wonderful things about Trastevere is the view from the Janiculum hill (Gianicolo). After walking up passeggiata del Gianicolo you are rewarded with spectacular views across Rome from the terrace, which is the largest in the city. The Orto Botanico (Botanical Garden) is here and is a great place to escape the chaos of the city.

Shops in Trastevere

Antica Caciara

The same family has run this cheese shop for over a hundred years. Now Anna and Rita Polica take care of the shop and Roberto keeps up the good work of his father and grandparents. Initially, shepherds brought in their Pecorino and ricotta from Ciociara, the area south of Rome, and these are still the shop's best sellers. Now they sell cheeses from all over Italy and you will find excellent mozzarella di bufala (traditional buffalo mozzarella) as well as the deliciously sinful burrata from Puglia. This looks like a money bag made of mozzarella, which releases a thick creamy liquid when cut.

VIA SAN FRANCISCO A RIPA 140, 06 581 2815

Ferrara

This tiny food store belongs to the same family which runs the nearby restaurant Enoteca Ferrara. If you know the restaurant, then you won't be surprised by the high quality of the olive oil, balsamic vinegar, wine, coffee, honey, cookies, and dried pasta sold here. It's a great place to pick up gourmet presents for yourself or fortunate friends.

VIA DEL MORO 3, 06 5833 3920

Forno la Renella

Although the name of the bakery has changed, the great one-hundred-year-old oven has not. The oven, which is never allowed to go out, is fired by hazelnut shells as well as wood, which give a great flavor and crisp crust to the loaves. The bakery is open every day of the week until late and Sunday brings food lovers from all over Rome to buy fresh, top-quality bread, biscotti, and takeout pizza with toppings such as tomato, olives, and oregano, and sliced potato and rosemary.

VIA DEL MORO 15, 06 581 7265

Giuliano Signorini

Chianina beef, from the most prized breed of cattle in Italy, is available at this butcher. Chianina cattle, which were originally from the Chiana valley in Tuscany, were bred by the Etruscans and Romans to sacrifice to their gods. Even the poet Virgil spoke of them with great respect in *The Georgics*. After World War II their fame spread as US servicemen returned home singing the praises of this excellent beef. Today, the cattle are exported for breeding and the first American chianina was born in 1972. As well as beef, the pork here is also highly recommended and Roman housewives order their oven-ready dishes in advance.

VIA SAN FRANCISCO A RIPA 50, 06 581 2764

Innocenti

Here, in the oldest pasticceria in Trastevere, tradition reigns supreme. Not for them international innovations. They specialize in cookies baked to authentic recipes with a large selection of well-loved favorites such as lingue di gatto (thin, crisp cookies) and paste di mandorla (almond cookies). The large apricot jam tarts are excellent.
VIA DELLA LUCE 21A, 06 580 3926

Innocenti

This is one of the most fascinating shops in Rome. As you walk in you are assailed by myriad aromas from the exotic imported spices, sacks of grains and pulses, and stacked ethnic ingredients. For baking there is a variety of flours, candied fruit, and nuts, and a good choice of organic supplies. There is also a wide selection of coffees and teas.
PIAZZA SAN COSIMATO 66, 06 581 2725

Laboratorio Trastevere

This is an essential address for late-night revelers in Trastevere. It has become a time-honored ritual to leave a party or discoteca and feast on cornetti (croissants) and other breakfast pastries straight from the oven in a bar such as this. Occasionally, an understandably morose insomniac or night-worker swells the youthful crowd.
VICOLO DEL CINQUE 40

Mercato Piazza San Cosimato

There is a small fruit and vegetable market in the central square, piazza San Cosimato, the heart of gastronomic Trastevere. Every morning except Sunday the stands are set up with colorful, seasonal fruit and vegetables. In the fall pumpkins and grotesque funghi porcini (ceps) take precedence, but in spring there are seemingly infinite shades of green on view as peas, fava (broad) beans, zucchini (courgettes), and asparagus (no white asparagus here) jostle for space. As the days get warmer, the air is perfumed with basil, and tomatoes and great red and yellow bell peppers elbow out the earlier greenery. Most eggplants (aubergines) are purple but in the summer the lilac and white variety makes an appearance. One year I saw small, pearly white melanzane and understood for the first time how the vegetable came to be named eggplant. There is a good fish stand but remember that fishermen do not work on Sunday, so don't expect fish on Monday.
PIAZZA SAN COSIMATO

La Norcineria Iacozzilli

The Umbrian town of Norcia had such a high reputation for the quality of its sausages and salami that shops selling these products became known as *norcinerie*. This historic butcher, whose owner is from Umbria, draws people from all areas of Rome because of the quality of its pork products, with many of the varieties of sausages made by the family. There's a great range of hams, and special cuts can be prepared to order. There is also a good selection of cheeses and dairy products, and on Fridays garbanzo beans (chickpeas) and salt cod.
VIA NATALE DEL GRANDE 15,
06 581 2734

Pages 68–9: Trastevere's atmospheric, narrow streets and numerous trattorias and restaurants are a draw for both Romans and visitors alike.

Valzani

Valzani is a legendary cake and chocolate shop that has been supplying cakes and desserts for special occasions since 1925. Traditional cakes such as sachertorte are still its mainstay, together with a good selection of chocolates, such as pralines filled with cinnamon, mint, or marzipan. The shop also sells pangiallo, a fat-free cake made with dry fruit, almonds, and hazelnuts. Another version of this cake is panpepato romano which is pangiallo with chocolate, honey, and spices.
VIA DEL MORO 37, 06 580 379

Spaghetti alle Vongole

Spaghetti with clams

Roman trattorias have taken this dish to their hearts, and it is probably on every menu on Fridays, and quite frequently on other days, too. The best clam is the *vongole verace*, but smaller ones are often substituted. The sauce is so good there is even a *povera* ("poor"), clamless version. There are two variations of the sauce, one with tomatoes and an *in bianco* version without.

SERVES 4
PREPARATION TIME: 10 MINUTES
COOKING TIME: 20 MINUTES

1kg/2¼lb large clams in the shell, scrubbed thoroughly	salt and freshly ground black pepper
4tbsp extra virgin olive oil	500g/1lb 2oz spaghetti
2 garlic cloves, chopped	handful of parsley, roughly chopped
1 chile pepper, crushed	
120ml/4fl oz/½ cup dry white wine	

Place the clams in a pan with 120ml/4fl oz/½ cup of water and cook over a high heat for 3–4 minutes (depending on the size of the clams), until the clams open; discard any that remain closed. Strain the cooking liquid through a sieve and put to one side.

Heat the olive oil in a large pan over a low heat and gently cook the garlic and chile pepper. When the garlic starts to change color, stir in the clams in their shells and add the reserved cooking liquid. Add the wine and simmer for a few minutes. Season with salt and pepper and keep warm.

Meanwhile, bring a large pan of lightly salted water to the boil, add the spaghetti, and cook according to the instructions on the pack until al dente. Drain and immediately add the spaghetti to the clams. Scatter with the parsley, toss well, and serve.

Stracciatella

Soup with "little rags"

I was amazed when I first tasted this soup at a christening in a small village just outside Rome. The eggs had been used while still warm from the hens, and the stock also had an impeccable pedigree. It was ambrosia. To get such a result, use only good home-made stock. You can prepare larger quantities of the stock than you need and freeze it. By adding herbs that you like just before using the stock, you can achieve a different flavor with the same basic stock. I find that chicken stock works best.

SERVES 4
PREPARATION TIME: 30 MINUTES, PLUS 2–3 HOURS FOR THE STOCK TO SIMMER
COOKING TIME: 15 MINUTES

	STOCK:
4 eggs	500g/1lb lean chicken or veal and bone
4tbsp freshly grated Parmesan cheese	1 onion, finely chopped
4tbsp semolina	2 carrots, chopped
salt and freshly ground black pepper	1 celery stick, chopped
pinch of freshly grated nutmeg	1 bay leaf
1 liter/1¾ pints/4⅓ cups good chicken, or veal stock	salt and freshly ground black pepper

First, prepare the stock. Put all the stock ingredients, apart from the salt and pepper, into a large pan and cover them with cold water. Bring this to the boil then reduce the heat and simmer for 2–3 hours. Strain, keeping only the liquid. Allow the stock to cool to room temperature before skimming off any fat which may have formed on the surface.

In a separate bowl beat the eggs with the Parmesan cheese, semolina, salt and pepper, and nutmeg. Add a ladleful of the stock.

In a large saucepan bring the remaining stock to the boil, and add salt and pepper, if desired. Remove from the heat and slowly whisk in the egg mixture, a tablespoonful at a time, until the soup is full of uniform egg and cheese threads. Simmer gently, whisking continuously for a few minutes, then add more salt and pepper, if desired, and serve immediately while the soup is still hot.

Restaurants in Trastevere

Alberto Ciarla

Alberto Ciarla is one of the great names in the Rome restaurant scene. In the late 1980s this was the first really professional fish restaurant in the city, providing consistently top quality food complemented by impeccable service and a superlative wine list. Today Alberto even works with the Italian government to ensure that high standards are maintained in Italian restaurants abroad. This is the place where Romans with a passion for good fish come for dinner. Dishes include fillet of sea bass with herbs, fillet of grouper with tomatoes and capers, grilled lobster, and even some raw fish dishes. As you would expect, the prices reflect the high quality of the dishes.

Piazza San Cosimato 40, 06 581 8668

Checco er Carrettiere

The Porcelli family has been at the same address since 1936. Like the city of Rome itself, the trattoria has survived many political and social vicissitudes to emerge triumphant. It has been the haunt of Rome's artistic figures, politicians, and soccer heroes, all of whom have come to eat authentic Roman food in good company. Today, the dishes are still traditional, although lightened a little to suit modern tastes, and fish has been added to the menu. Dishes include coda alla vaccinara, carciofi alla romana, ravioli, and rice croquettes known as supplì. One of the sons runs an elegant bar serving pastries and drinks in the old milk store next door.

Via Benedetta 10, 06 581 9668

Enoteca Ferrara

If you love good wine then this is the place for you. The wine lists are the size of telephone directories (there is one for white wines and one for reds). The two sisters who run the restaurant, Mary and Lina, have their roots in Campania, which goes part of the way to explaining the intriguing combinations of vegetables and seafood. An interesting soup made with a very old variety of wheat, zuppa di farro, makes an unusual first course. The bar at the entrance is open from 6pm, and for a reasonable price, you can enjoy a glass of good wine and some small culinary delights.

Piazza Trilussa 1, 06 5833 3920

Le Mani in Pasta

A young team runs this small trattoria (open every day except Monday) on the quiet side of Trastevere, near piazza Santa Cecilia. They use good quality ingredients in interesting ways to produce dishes like gnocchi with radicchio and clams. The menu is small but excellent value. The main dining room is also small, although an added illusion of space is given by the view into the kitchen beyond.

Via dei Genovesi 37, 06 581 6017

Osteria der Belli

As you would expect from an osteria, the decor is simple, but the food is of a consistently high standard. Highlights of the menu include the delicious spaghetti with mussels or clams, and straightforward fish dishes at fair prices, such as rombo al forno (baked turbot). Monday is the day of rest.

Piazza San Apollonia 9/10, 06 580 3782

Ivo a Trastevere

Ivo has been popular for many years. Every day of the week except Tuesdays, young people push themselves into the bustling, busy space as they jostle to eat the superlative pizza at this family-run trattoria. Although the father has retired, the mother and son keep the pizza coming, and the other dishes are good too.

Via San Francisco a Ripa 158, 06 581 7082

Paris

Nothing seems to have changed here for years, except the prices, which have got a little steeper. It is in a handy location and is one of the few restaurants near piazza Santa Maria that is always reliable. Good fresh fish and typically Roman dishes like pasta alla Matriciana and carciofi alla giudia are on the menu. In warmer weather, there are tables outside in piazza San Calisto — ideal for watching the world go by.

PIAZZA SAN CALISTO 7A, 06 581 5378

Sora Lella

The fascinating setting on Isola Tiberina is one of the reasons for coming here, especially at lunchtime when the light on the water is magical. Try to get a table by the window. The food has improved lately, accompanied, unfortunately, by a similar increase in prices. Typical Roman dishes are well prepared, such as rolled slices of meat with bell peppers, and tonnarelli alla cuccagna (pasta with sausage, bacon, and walnuts).

PONTE QUATTRO CAPI 16, 06 686 1601

Trattoria degli Amici

This friendly trattoria is run along cooperative lines, with many of the staff working as volunteers. They are very professional and the prevailing mood of staff and clients is lively and warm, as the name "trattoria of friends" would suggest. The menu offers Roman specialties, such as the ubiquitous pasta alla Matriciana and zuppa di ceci, but also dishes from other regions, like trofie al pesto (small pasta twists with pesto). In good weather you can eat outside in the small historic square.

PIAZZA DI SANT'EGIDIO 5, 06 580 6033

Panattoni

Be prepared to queue for a table at this popular evening pizzeria, which is known affectionately as the obitorio (mortuary) by regulars because of the great slabs of marble on the long tables. The room is simple and could be bleak were it not for the liveliness of the customers and the relaxed, happy, convivial atmosphere. Although a sign says that the pizza is made in the Neapolitan way, it is in fact Roman style, thin and crisp.

VIALE TRASTEVERE 53/57, 06 580 0919

Involtini di Carne e Carciofi

Meat and artichoke rolls

I learned this recipe many years ago from Rome's historic restaurant Checcino dal 1887 in Testaccio. Over the years, like all cooks, I have gradually strayed from their original recipe and changed the proportions to suit my own taste.

SERVES 4
PREPARATION TIME: 1 HOUR, PLUS 2–3 HOURS FOR THE STOCK
TO SIMMER
COOKING TIME: 30 MINUTES

3tbsp extra virgin olive oil
1 onion, finely chopped
4 artichokes, trimmed and
    sliced (see Spaghetti ai
    Carciofi recipe)
1 floury potato, thinly sliced
1tbsp chopped fresh parsley
120ml/4fl oz/½ cup dry white
    wine

salt and freshly ground
    black pepper
8 thin slices of veal, chicken,
    or turkey breast
1 liter/1¾ pints/4⅓ cups light
    chicken, or veal stock,
    boiling (see Stracciatella)

Heat half the oil in a large skillet and gently fry the onion until soft. Stir in the artichokes and potato, then after a few minutes the parsley, wine, a little of the boiling stock, and some salt and pepper. Cover and simmer gently, stirring occasionally until the vegetables are tender. Drain, reserving the cooking liquid, and transfer the vegetables to a blender or food processor. Purée the vegetables until they form a smooth sauce.

Place each slice of meat, in turn, between two sheets of plastic wrap and beat with a rolling pin to flatten. They should be about ½ cm/⅕ inch thick. Remove the plastic wrap. Season the meat and place a spoonful of the vegetable purée at one end of each piece. Roll up from a narrow end to form a small cylinder, and tie into shape with kitchen string.

Heat the remaining oil in a skillet set over a medium heat and gently brown the meat rolls. Arrange with the seam underneath, in a single layer.

Pour the remaining stock and vegetable purée over the meat rolls. Simmer gently for about 30 minutes, turning the rolls once or twice, or until the meat is tender. Add a little water if needed during the cooking, but the sauce should be fairly thick.

Lift the rolls from the pan, cut away the kitchen string, and serve the rolls with the sauce.

Pollo alla Romana

Chicken with bell peppers and tomatoes

This dish is often served with red bell peppers, which give a sweet flavor to the chicken, but green bell peppers with their distinctive bitter tang are more authentic. A whole chicken should be used to gain flavor; if you substitute all breast meat you will get a much blander dish.

SERVES 4

PREPARATION TIME: 15 MINUTES

COOKING TIME: 1 HOUR

4tbsp olive oil

50g/2oz/¼ cup bacon, chopped

2 garlic cloves, minced

1 chicken, cut into serving pieces

120ml/4fl oz/½ cup dry white wine, preferably Frascati

500g/1lb 2oz full-flavored red tomatoes, or canned Italian tomatoes, chopped

3 green bell peppers, cored, seeded and cut into strips

salt and freshly ground black pepper

Heat the oil in a heavy-bottomed pan and gently fry the bacon for 5–10 minutes until the fat runs. Add the garlic and chicken pieces and cook until the chicken is lightly browned. Then pour in the wine and continue to cook gently for a further 5 minutes.

Stir the tomatoes and peppers into the pan, season with salt and pepper, and cook uncovered over a low heat for about 45 minutes. Stir the mixture every 10 minutes to stop it sticking to the base of the pan.

Tagliatelle Cacio e Pepe

Tagliatelle with Pecorino cheese and black pepper

This is a great Roman favorite, dating back to the *cucina povera* tradition. It can be prepared with any pasta, although tagliatelle or a slimmer version called tonnarelli works best.

SERVES 4
PREPARATION TIME: 5 MINUTES
COOKING TIME: 10 MINUTES

500g/1lb 2oz tagliatelle
salt and freshly ground
  black pepper

100g/3½oz Pecorino Romano
  cheese
handful of flat-leaf parsley,
  finely chopped

Bring a large saucepan of lightly salted water to the boil. You will only need a little salt because Pecorino Romano cheese is very salty. Drop the pasta into the boiling water and stir once. Cook for 6–9 minutes, or according to the packet instructions.

Grate the Pecorino as the pasta is cooking. Before the pasta is fully cooked, remove a ladleful of the pasta water and mix with half the Pecorino in a blender to make a smooth sauce.

Roughly drain the pasta and toss with the Pecorino sauce. Sprinkle with the remaining cheese and season with black pepper. Serve on warm plates, garnished with chopped parsley.

Cozze Gratinate

Baked stuffed mussels in their shells

Versions of this dish are found in every region of Italy. I particularly like this Roman one, especially with the addition of minced fresh ginger, which gives it a modern-day twist.

SERVES 4
PREPARATION TIME: 30 MINUTES
COOKING TIME: 7 MINUTES

handful of flat-leaf parsley
4 garlic cloves, peeled
1tsp minced fresh ginger
  (optional)
40g/1½oz/¾ cup fresh
  breadcrumbs
salt and freshly ground
  black pepper

1kg/2¼lb mussels in their
  shells, cleaned
2tbsp olive oil
1 lemon, cut into wedges,
  to serve

Preheat the broiler (grill) to a high heat. Finely chop the parsley, garlic, and ginger, if using, together and mix with the breadcrumbs and seasoning.

Scrub the mussels, removing the "beard" and any encrustations, and put them with a little water into a large pan. Cover the pan and put it over a high heat for about 4 minutes, or until the shells open; discard any mussels that remain closed.

When the mussels are cool enough to handle, remove the top shells from half of them. Then place all the mussels on a baking sheet, arranging those on the half shells with the meat uppermost. Spoon the breadcrumb mixture over the mussels, covering them completely. Sprinkle with the olive oil, then place under the hot broiler for 2–3 minutes until the crumb mix is crisp and golden. Serve immediately with lemon wedges.

Landmarks

Isola Tiberina, the island in the River Tiber, is a good stepping stone on the way to or from Trastevere. There is even a good restaurant here for lunch, Sora Lella. From the Ghetto area, take Ponte Fabricio, a footbridge dating from 62 BC (below), to the island, then make your way up via della Lungaretta to the church of Santa Maria in Trastevere.

Gianicolo

At the far boundary of Trastevere is the Gianicolo (Janiculum Hill), which you reach by walking up via Garibaldi. An equestrian statue of the great man himself, Giuseppe Garibaldi, stands at the ridge where he made a historic stand against the superior French forces in 1849. Anita Garibaldi, his fiery Brazilian wife, has her statue further down the hill. She is shown controlling a skittish horse while cradling a baby in one arm and a shotgun in the other! On the Gianicolo is the Orto Botanico, a lovely, peaceful botanical garden, but the main reason to come up the hill is for the view. From here you can see all of Rome and on a clear day you can even make out the villages to the south, the Castelli Romani. In the height of summer it is a welcome, cool retreat from the shimmering heat of the city.

Isola Tiberina

The island has a fascinating history. In 291 BC Rome was suffering from a particularly severe epidemic, so envoys went to Epidaurus in Greece to ask for help from the god of healing, Asclepius. One of the sacred snakes slithered after the envoys and on to their boat, which was seen as a favorable sign from the god. When back in Rome the snake settled on the island and a temple was built on the spot. Travertine prows were added to the island to commemorate the ship that the snake had sailed on.

In the tenth century the church of San Bartolomeo was built on the ruins of the old temple. Rahere, court jester to England's King Henry II, was cured of malaria here, and returned to London to found St.

Bartholemew's Hospital. In 1538 a hospital was established on the island and the monks had an alms box labeled *"Fate bene, fratelli"* ("Do good, brothers"). Over the years the good work of the alms givers has become attributed to the monks and today the hospital is known as the "Fatebenefratelli" or "The brothers who do good".

Santa Maria in Trastevere

The heart of the area is Santa Maria in Trastevere (right), one of the finest medieval churches in Rome, and believed to be the oldest church in the city. It was founded by Pope Callixtus I in the third century, before Christianity was widely accepted. The present church dates from the twelfth century, with columns taken from ruins of ancient Roman buildings. The mosaics on the facade show Mary feeding the infant Jesus, and ten young women holding lamps; they are believed to be the wise and foolish virgins.

Villa Farnesina

The beautiful Renaissance villa is well worth visiting (mornings only) for its lovely interior and magical gardens. It was built in 1508 by Baldassare Chigi as a suburban villa. Since the Farnese family bought it in 1580, it has been known as the Villa Farnesina. On the ground floor are the Loggia of Galatea, with a stunning fresco by Raphael of the triumph of Galatea, and the Loggia of Cupid and Psyche. The Salone delle Prospettive on the upper floor, is decorated with a trompe l'oeil fresco by Baldassare Peruzzi.

Pages 78–9: this vibrant, ornate ceiling is in Villa Farnesina. The villa was bought by the Farnese family in the sixteenth century.

Piazza di Spagna & Via Veneto

Here among some of Rome's best-known landmarks, such as the Trevi Fountain and the Spanish Steps, you are still in the historic heart of the city. One of Rome's top restaurants, Dal Bolognese, sits at the northern end of via del Corso on beautiful piazza del Popolo, bounded by churches rich in art treasures. Historic Antico Caffè Greco has been serving coffee to Romans and English Romantic poets alike since the eighteenth century, and a visit to San Crispino for one of their delicious ice creams is a Roman experience not to be missed.

Piazza di Spagna & Via Veneto

Rome has many faces: there is archaeological Rome, ecclesiastical Rome, and fashionable Rome. In this area they are all represented, with diplomatic Rome and historical Rome added as well. It was the great ambition of Napoleon to be a second Augustus and he named his son and heir "King of Rome". Napoleon's family is inextricably connected to Rome. His mother, Letizia, made her home here after Waterloo and his sister, Paulina, who was married to Prince Borghese, kept Rome entertained and scandalized for many years. Her famous nude statue by Canova is in the Borghese Museum.

Ara Pacis, the Altar of Peace, is a major work from the Augustan Golden Age and is probably one of the most important Roman finds. It is decorated with grand friezes with life-size figures depicting Augustus, his family, and his officials. Augustus's daughter, Julia, was married to Marcus Agrippa and so we see the figure of the man who built so many aqueducts and fountains and whose name appears on the Pantheon's pediment. The small child is Augustus's grandson, Lucius. Near this great monument is Augustus's mausoleum, surrounded by cypress trees. Octavia's son, Marcellus, was the first member of the family to be buried here.

Via Lucullo, off via Veneto, is named after the Roman epicure Lucullus, who amassed huge wealth serving as proconsul in Asia. When he returned to Rome he retired from public life and devoted himself to pleasure. He built many luxurious villas all over Italy, but his masterpiece was the great garden that covered most of the area surrounding via Veneto. He is even credited with introducing Rome to cherries, which he brought back from his travels in Asia.

The Quirinale Palace, once the summer residence of the Popes, has been the scene of many dramas involving the power of the Papal States. In 1798 when Pope Pius VI refused to renounce temporal power, Napoleon had him snatched from the palace and taken to France. In 1809 the Papal States were officially annexed by the French Empire. Pius excommunicated Napoleon but had to wait until the emperor was confined to St. Helena before he could return to Rome and power.

The great entrance to piazza del Popolo was built to welcome the Swedish Queen Christina who became a Catholic and abdicated her throne in 1654 before coming to live in Rome. The exiled Stuart royal family also made their home here.

Via Margutta used to be the artists' quarter and would-be models posed on the Spanish Steps, hoping for work. Piazza di Spagna was the center for foreign writers and musicians in the nineteenth century; nowadays, history and fashion come together for this is the area for fashion. Designer names such as Valentino have their ateliers here, while others such as Ferragamo and Gucci have their shops in via dei Condotti (which gets its name from the aqueduct conduits), as do expensive jewelers and fashion stores.

The other parallel streets have their own characters. The narrower via delle Carrozze is where the great coaches that brought travelers doing the Grand Tour of Europe were overhauled and repaired. Some of Rome's most elegant restaurants are in this area, perhaps bringing to mind memories of Lucullus's extravagant feasts, and in via della Croce there is a collection of small specialty food shops, and a little street market selling fruit and vegetables.

Shops in Piazza di Spagna & Via Veneto

Fratelli Ciavatta

It is difficult to find serious food shops in a zone overrun with tourism like the Fontana di Trevi area, but in this courteous store you can be certain of buying top quality products, such as prosciutto, cheese and other dairy products, bread, and wine. Simply walk on home to an excellent lunch with what you've bought.

Via del Lavatore 31, 06 679 2935

Fratelli Fabbri

There is an excellent salumeria section in this grocery store and a small selection of prepared dishes such as stuffed tomatoes and Parmesan baked eggplant (aubergine) and pasta. When you see that they also sell bread, pasta, and wine, your lunch or dinner is taken care of.

Via della Croce 27, No telephone

Luigi di Angelis

This is a butcher's shop with a difference. Other grocery items are on sale as well as the great quality meat, and this is the only shop I know where you can buy poulet de Bresse (very good quality chicken from Bresse in France). In season there is a wide choice of game, and there are ready-prepared meat dishes as well as universal favorites such as pasta al forno (baked pasta).

Via Flavia 74, 06 4201 2192

Primizie e Verdura di Luca Persiani

In Rome today there are few good greengrocers because the advent of small central supermarkets has elbowed them out. Many areas have become vegetable and fruit deserts when the street markets shut at lunchtime. But in via Flavia, this excellent shop still flourishes, selling reliable, fresh produce which they will wash and trim on request. Pots of herbs and some exotic fruit to liven up the seasonal choice are also available.

Via Flavia 36, 06 474 3726

Puntari

Puntari started life as a good bakery and the bread is still excellent, as are the focaccia and pizza. It was natural to expand to cakes and cookies, but the enterprising owners have gone further, adding a salumeria, and a rosticceria to sell roast chicken, and serving other tempting morsels, such as supplì (savory rice croquettes), and stuffed tomatoes.

Via Flavia 48, 06 481 8225

Annibale

People travel from all over Rome to buy the high quality meat at Annibale. The lamb and kid come from carefully selected producers and there is both Danish and Tuscan beef. All the ingredients for the quinto quarto (dishes made from a variety of meats and off-cuts) can be found here and there are cuts for specific dishes like bollito misto (boiled mixed meats, chicken, and sausage). On Saturday mornings there is an extra incentive to visit the shop: customers are offered slices of delicious warm porchetta (suckling pig), a specialty from Ariccia in the Castelli Romani. There are several ready-prepared dishes for those in a rush.

Via di Ripetta 236, 06 361 2269

La Stadera

This tiny fish shop is open all day on Tuesday, Thursday, and Friday, but only in the morning on Wednesday and Saturday. It is the only fish shop in the immediate vicinity, so if you want something specific it is good idea to come early in the day. The fish is excellent and the prices are surprisingly fair considering you are in the heart of an expensive neighborhood.
VIA DELLA CROCE 71A, 06 679 2683

Teichner

San Lorenzo in Lucina is a lovely pedestrianized square dating back to the twelfth century and any excuse to come here is welcome. Teichner provides just that, being a gastronomic heaven where you can buy everything needed for a great meal. The salumeria section has cold cuts of excellent quality and there are extravagant specialties like balsamic vinegar in Consorzio bottles, caviar, and foie gras. The shop is open all day, which is a boon for people in a hurry, and there are small tables where you can sit and eat some of the tempting things on sale.
PIAZZA SAN LORENZO IN LUCINA 17, 06 687 1449

San Crispino

When San Crispino first opened in 1993 the face of Rome gelaterias was changed. One revolutionary move was to abolish cones, because the owners thought the poor quality ruined the taste of the ice cream. Similarly, you won't find any chocolate sauces or artificial preservatives. Their ice cream contains no artificial ingredients, so the colors are natural and are therefore paler than those of many other ice creams. The crema San Crispino is made with honey, and there are more unusual flavors such as licorice, ginger, and cinnamon.
VIA DELLA PANETTERIA 42, 06 679 3924

L'Arte del Caffè

If you go anywhere in Italy, people will tell you that the best pizza comes from Naples and the best coffee from Rome. The reason Roman coffee is considered to be so good is not just because of the quality of the coffee beans, but also the quality of the water. The dominance of Italian-style coffee has made words like *cappuccino* and *espresso* recognizable worldwide, but for a genuine Roman coffee in a historic setting, the bars Sant'Eustachio and Tazza d'Oro are hard to beat.

At the beginning of the seventeenth century coffee was known in Europe as the "wine of Arabia". It was not until 1683, when the Turks were defeated in their attempts to capture Vienna and left behind several sacks of coffee as they retreated, that a large quantity of coffee was seen in Europe. Austrians quickly took to drinking coffee, often accompanied by sweet pastries called *kipfel*, that were crescent-shaped in celebration of their victory over the Turks.

By the end of the century coffee houses were opening in other European capitals, and the first Italian coffee house was Florian's in Venice, soon to be followed by Caffè Greco in Rome. Carlo Goldoni, the eighteenth-century playwright, captured the Italian coffee house scene in his play *La Bottega del Caffè*. However, it was the invention of the espresso machine that changed coffee drinking, and now Italian-style coffee is drunk around the world.

Most Romans cannot function until they have had their morning "fix", and each Roman has his personal preference and his favorite bar. What many non-Italians call espresso, in Italy is simply un caffè, although some Romans will only drink it *in vetro* (in a small glass) in the morning. Then there are those who order it *macchiato*, stained with milk. A double ration is *un doppio*, while a *caffè lungo* is diluted with more water. Early in the cold mornings those setting off to do hard physical work often ask for a *caffè corretto*, coffee "corrected" by having a stiff shot of grappa or brandy added. There are even more variations with milk. A *latte macchiato* is hot milk "stained" with coffee, and a cappuccino is known all over the world, although an Italian would never order it after a meal, only in the morning. That is why you will struggle to find a really hot cappuccino, because people want to gulp it down and run. If you don't want a tepid cappuccino ask for it *bollente* (boiling). In Rome many people order their cappuccino *senza schiuma*, without froth, or a caffè latte in a glass with more milk than a cup could hold. I am always amused when a visitor complains bitterly that they ordered a latte and a glass of milk arrived.

To make good coffee you need good quality, freshly roasted, and freshly ground beans, and a machine that is cleaned daily. You also need a skilled operator — the Illy coffee family says that the importance of the human hand cannot be overestimated. Many barmen like to add their own personal touch, sprinkling chocolate on the froth of the cappuccino in the shape of a heart.

For the best coffee in the center of Rome there are two historic bars near the Pantheon that are always packed with coffee fiends. Sant'Eustachio, which serves a tempting coffee granita with cream in summer, and Tazza d'Oro, whose specialty is monachella, a cappuccino with cream.

Sant'Eustachio, Piazza Sant'Eustachio 82
Tazza d'Oro, Via degli Orfani 84

La Vignarola

Artichokes, peas, and fava (broad) beans

Vignarola can only be prepared for the short time each year in late spring and early summer when fava beans, peas, and artichokes are all in season.

SERVES 4
PREPARATION TIME: 20 MINUTES
COOKING TIME: 20 MINUTES

4 artichokes	salt and freshly ground
2tbsp olive oil	black pepper
1 leek, finely chopped	500g/1lb 2oz fava (broad)
small handful of mint,	beans, shelled
roughly chopped	500g/1lb 2oz peas, shelled

Remove the tough outside leaves from each artichoke and, using a sharp knife, cut two-thirds off the top of each artichoke. Cut the artichokes into quarters, removing the choke and trimming round the outside until you are left with a few of the outside leaves and the heart.

Heat the oil in a large pan and add the leek. Add the artichokes and mint, and season with salt and pepper. Cover the pan and cook over a low heat for about 15 minutes.

Add the beans and peas, and 1–2 tablespoons of water if the pan looks dry. Cook until the vegetables are soft and the liquid has almost disappeared.

Broccoli "Strascinati" in Padella

Roman-style broccoli

In Rome this dish traditionally uses the pungent green *broccolo Romano* (sold outside Italy as Romanesco cauliflower). The term "strascinati", which translates as "dragged into the skillet", suggests that the dish should be made with the freshest produce available. The recipe works equally well with cauliflower, or a mixture of broccoli and cauliflower.

SERVES 4
PREPARATION TIME: 10 MINUTES
COOKING TIME: 5 MINUTES

500g/1lb 2oz broccoli	1 chile pepper, crushed with
4tbsp extra virgin olive oil	the back of a knife
2 garlic cloves, minced	salt

Trim the broccoli, discarding the tough stalks and outer leaves. Divide into small florets or sprigs.

Heat the oil in a large pan with a lid and stir in the broccoli, garlic, chile pepper, and a little salt. Cover and cook very gently, stirring frequently. It may be necessary to add a sprinkling of water toward the end if the broccoli looks a little dry, but the best results come from a judicious combination of frying and steaming. Do not drown the vegetables.

Serve immediately, either alone or as an accompaniment to broiled (grilled) meats.

Al Moro

This historic restaurant has the feel of an elegant trattoria. The menu does not change and people come here to enjoy their favorite dishes. The spaghetti al moro is a carbonara with peperoncino (chile peppers) and the excellent spaghetti alle vongole (with clams) has a subtle "extra". In the fall the lamb and the tagliolini with white truffles are the highlights of the menu.

VICOLO DELLE BOLLETTE 13, 06 678 3495

Al Presidente

The Allegrini family has made this a reliably popular restaurant. Sebastiano and his sister, Ludovica, look after the restaurant with charming attentiveness, while mother Daniela is in charge in the kitchen. For cooking the Allegrinis use only their own olive oil, which comes from the Sabine hills north of Rome. There is a shorter "tasting" menu, chosen to satisfy most tastes. Antipasti include fried slivers of squid, bell peppers, and zucchini (courgettes), and to follow there is a masterly paccheri con sugo di scorfano (pasta with a scorpion fish sauce). Traditional pastas such as Matriciana are handled with equal competence. The presentation of the dishes is elegant and the desserts are enticing — for example, the little tray with crema caramella.

VIA IN ARCIONE 95, 06 679 7342

Dal Bolognese

This restaurant, which sits on piazza del Popolo, one of Rome's most beautiful (and prestigious) piazzas, is at the top of visiting gourmets "must visit" list. Most of the other clients are regulars who return to enjoy their favorite dishes and perhaps to be tempted into trying something different. Different, not new, because here tradition reigns. As the name suggests, this restaurant specializes in dishes from the Bologna region: tagliatelle with a genuine ragù (ground beef sauce), or bollito misto (mixed boiled meats) with its salsa verde (uncooked green sauce with anchovies, herbs, capers, olive oil, and lemon), and mostarda di frutta (mixed fruit pickle). There are also some dishes from other regions, and in summer there is a terrace for outdoor dining.

PIAZZA DEL POPOLO 72, 06 361 1426

Antico Caffè Greco

Caffè Greco, a historic bar which has been here since 1760, can boast several English Romantic poets, Goethe and Liszt, among other illustrious customers. Today the entrance is thronged with people standing to enjoy a quick coffee, while in the comfortable little rooms at the back you can have a swift snack or a longer aperitivo.

Via Condotti 86, 06 679 1700

Le Colline Emiliane

Nothing changes in this long-established restaurant because the regular customers love the menu as it is. Fresh pasta is served in many guises; the stuffed tortelli is particularly good, but then so is the tagliolini with prosciutto, making choosing difficult. For a main course, duck with orange is a firm favorite.

Via Avignonesi 22, 06 481 7538

Il Margutta

Via Margutta is a fascinating street behind via del Babuino, one of the three main arteries leading off piazza del Popolo. It has rows of artists' studios with lush gardens, and was once the bohemian quarter. The studios are now fashionably expensive but the street has retained its "other world" atmosphere. In this vegetarian restaurant cut off from the frenzy of Roman traffic, calm reigns, and you can sit back and enjoy an antipasto such as the carpaccio of artichokes with nuts, grated celery, and Parmesan shavings. Follow with a primo of stuffed tortelloni in a pumpkin broth and a secondo of polenta with winter vegetables and ricotta di Bufala, accompanied by an organic wine or beer.

Via Margutta 82, 06 323 1025

Papa Baccus

Tagliolini with prosciutto, delicate tortelloni (square filled pasta shapes) stuffed with potato, and little crostini with toppings of pâté or vegetables are examples of the high quality food that is served for dinner in this small, elegant Tuscan restaurant just off via Veneto. As Tuscany has a long coastline, it is not surprising to find a fine example of cacciuccio alla livornese (Livornese fish soup with red mullet, shellfish, and tomatoes). Another popular dish is tagliato di manzo (steak seared quickly, then sliced and finished in a hot oven with herbs and olive oil). There are a few tables outside where you can dine in the warmer months.

Via Toscana 36, 06 4274 2808

Pizza l'Archetto

This is a useful place to know near the Trevi Fountain where you can eat a decent pizza or plate of pasta after seeing a play or a movie. There is a good selection of bruschetta and there are plenty of spaghetti sauces to choose from, such as pecorara, stuffed zucchini (courgette) flowers, or clam and capers.

Via del Archetto 26, 06 678 9064

Rosati

Rosati opened in the early part of the last century and it still retains an air of elegance. From early morning to late at night you can enjoy good coffee and cornetti (croissants), light meals, and snacks, and aperitivi or wine with delicious nibbles. There are tables outside where you can sit and watch the world. In the 1960s "celebrity spotting" was a favorite pastime, but today the piazza has regained its tranquility and you can enjoy a quiet drink.

Piazza del Popolo 4, 06 322 5859

Tullio

A warm, welcoming atmosphere pervades this traditional trattoria just off piazza Barberini. There are many Tuscan specialties on the menu such as fagioli al fiasca (white beans cooked in a flask), and pappardelle with game sauce, although over the years some Roman dishes have crept in too.

Via San Nicola da Tolentino 26, 06 474 5560

Garofolato in Sugo di Umido
Beef pot roast with cloves

This great Roman dish is named after the clove, *garofono*, that flavors the meat. The rich sauce that is made from the cooking juices, known as *sugo di umido*, used to be served with pasta, with the meat reserved for another meal, in typical *cucina povera* style. Today, the meat and sauce are usually served together, with extra sauce being eagerly mopped up with coarse bread, *pane casereccia*. The half slices of the oval bread resemble the heel of a flat shoe.

SERVES 4
PREPARATION TIME: 30 MINUTES
COOKING TIME: 2–2½ HOURS

1kg/2¼lb piece of beef, usually rump roast (topside)
50g/2oz prosciutto, cut into thin strips
1 garlic clove, cut into slivers
6 cloves
salt and freshly ground black pepper
1tbsp olive oil

1 onion, peeled and diced
1 carrot, sliced
1 celery stick, sliced
2 ripe tomatoes, peeled and chopped
fresh marjoram or parsley, roughly chopped
225ml/8fl oz/1 cup red wine

Make deep cuts into the meat and insert the strips of prosciutto, using a larding needle if available. If not, use a skewer to push in the strips of prosciutto. Make a row of incisions along the length of the meat and insert slivers of garlic alternated with cloves. Season with salt and pepper.

Heat the oil in a Dutch oven (casserole dish), add the meat, and brown it quickly. Put the onion, carrot, celery, tomatoes, and herbs around the meat and pour over the wine. Bring to a boil, then simmer until the wine has reduced by half.

Add enough boiling water to just cover the meat. Cover the pan and cook very gently for 1½–2 hours. Remove the meat from the pan and keep warm.

Purée the vegetables and cooking liquid, which should produce a dense, rich brown sauce. Cut the meat into thick slices and spoon over the sauce.

Carciofi alla Romana
Braised mint-stuffed artichokes

In Rome in the fall artichokes tinged with purple, *violette*, are available, but in spring the large round romaneschi artichokes from around Cerveteri come into season, and these are used for carciofi alla Romana. Traditionally, they are stuffed with wild *mentuccia* (pennyroyal), but I prefer to use the true mint, known here as *menta Romana*.

SERVES 6
PREPARATION TIME: 30 MINUTES
COOKING TIME: 1 HOUR

6 artichokes
1 lemon, halved
juice of 1 lemon
2 garlic cloves, finely chopped
1tbsp chopped fresh parsley
3tbsp chopped fresh mint

salt
6tbsp olive oil
120ml/4fl oz/½ cup dry white wine (optional)*
6tbsp boiling water

Remove the tough outer leaves of the artichokes, and trim the stalks, leaving at least 5cm/2 inches of stalk.

Using a very sharp knife, pare off the coarse upper part of the leaves while turning the artichoke round in your hand. At the end of this the artichoke should be almost tulip shaped. Rub the artichoke with half a lemon at regular intervals to prevent discoloration. Cut off the tips of the "tulips" so that the artichokes can stand on their heads. As it is prepared put each artichoke into a bowl of lemon juice and water.

In a small bowl, mix the garlic and herbs with a little salt and about 1 tablespoon of the olive oil. Taking one artichoke at a time, force open the leaves and remove the coarse choke (known in Italian as *pelo*), with a teaspoon. Spoon a little of the herb mixture into the cavity. Prepare all the artichokes in this way, then put them in a deep pan large enough to fit all the artichokes in one layer with the stalks pointing upwards. Pour in the rest of the oil, the wine if using, half a lemon, a little salt and the boiling water. Cover and cook gently for 1 hour. Remove from the pan and allow to cool to room temperature before serving.

* If wine isn't used, substitute more boiling water.

Landmarks

This area has world-famous landmarks, including fountains, palaces, piazzas, and ancient Roman monuments. To take in these sights on foot, you would begin at Palazzo del Quirinale, the presidential palace, and then head north taking in the Trevi Fountain and the Spanish Steps, arriving in vast piazza del Popolo. Here the Church of Santa Maria del Popolo contains exceptional works of art by Raphael and Caravaggio.

Ara Pacis Augustae

This fascinating monument is a great altar built to celebrate Augustus's triumphal return to Rome after campaigns in Gaul and Spain, and to commemorate the peace he had established throughout the Roman world. It is made of fine white marble from Carrara and shows life-like carvings of Augustus and his family. The first panels were dug up in the sixteenth century and further pieces have been found over the years. It was not until 1938 that the altar was painstakingly pieced together and the gaps filled with copies.

Fontana del Tritone & Fontana delle Ape

In piazza Barberini, Bernini's Triton Fountain, commissioned in 1642 by Pope Urban VIII, is marooned in a sea of traffic. Four dolphins with their tails in the air support a huge scallop shell on which sits a triton. On the corner with via Veneto, the Fountain of the Bees, shows bees (the emblem of the Barberini family) drinking from a scallop shell.

Fontana di Trevi

The baroque Trevi Fountain (below), the most spectacular fountain in Rome, completely dominates the little piazza. Designed by Nicola Salvi in the eighteenth century, it depicts Neptune riding his shell-shaped chariot, along with sculptures of real and mythological sea creatures. Every day visitors follow tradition by throwing coins over their shoulder into the water to ensure they return.

Palazzo del Quirinale

The Quirinale Palace, high on the hill, has been the official home of the Italian president since 1870. Before then it was the summer residence of the Popes, before being used by the kings of Italy, who decorated the rooms with elaborate tapestries. Inside there is a cycle of frescos by Guido Reni in the Chapel of the Annuncation, while the Pauline Chapel, similar in size to the Sistine Chapel in the Vatican, is decorated with stucco work by Martino Ferrabosco. Outside, the figures of Castor and Pollux dominate the square.

Pages 96–7: the sculptures in Fontana di Trevi are full of symbolism. The agitated horse represents stormy seas, while the figure blowing into a conch represents the calm sea.

Piazza del Popolo

Via del Corso ends in the beautiful, open, oval-shaped piazza del Popolo (below). The seventeenth-century twin churches of Santa Maria dei Miracoli and Santa Maria di Monte Santo stand on either side of via del Corso. The focal point of the piazza is the Egyptian obelisk of Pharaoh Rameses II, which has four marble lions spouting water at its base. At the far end, the great Porta di Popolo, modeled on a Roman triumphal arch, leads to via Flaminia, a long road which was begun in 220 BC to link Rome and the Adriatic coast.

Piazza di Spagna

Piazza di Spagna, although thronged with tourists at all times of the year, still has the ability to impress. Young people sit around the basin of the Barcaccia (the fountain at the foot of the steps which resembles a half-sunk boat), and little groups of people sit at various levels on the great Spanish Steps leading up to the Trinità dei Monti, the church built by King Charles VIII of France in 1494. The piazza gained its name when the Spanish ambassador to the Holy See had his headquarters here in the sixteenth century.

Via Veneto

The American Embassy is on via Veneto in majestic, amber-colored Palazzo Margherita. This area was once part of the Ludovisi estate before the land was sold in 1879 to provide prestigious sites for the buildings needed for the capital of the new republic. In fact, the Ludovisi spent so much money building the palazzo that they over-extended themselves and could not afford to live there. In the 1960s via Veneto was the hub of la dolce vita. It was the smartest place to see and be seen, and film stars and celebrities abounded.

Piazza Venezia, Via Nazionale & San Lorenzo

This area encompasses many different faces of Rome, from the ancient Roman baths complex, the Terme di Diocleziano, through to the vibrant student hub of San Lorenzo. Although this area is not the city's best known district for food, you'll still find one of the finest wine shops in the city, Enoteca Trimani, as well as a small but historic *pescheria* which supplies Rome's best fish restaurants, and a branch of the famous high quality grocery store Roscioli. Ancient Romans came here to do their food shopping at the Mercati Traianei (right) — six floors of markets and stores selling everything from spices to seafood.

Piazza Venezia, Via Nazionale & San Lorenzo

In this part of the city you get a feeling for everyday life as you pass from the Rome of the caesars to the modern face of Rome today. The remains of Trajan's market, which was built at the beginning of the first century AD, dominates the western edge of this area. It was built as a group of commercial buildings on six different street levels, and gives a vivid picture of how people lived in Trajan's time. The complex, which acted like an ancient Roman shopping mall, had a covered shopping arcade, an apartment block, inns, and more than 150 shops.

When you explore the narrow streets between via IV Novembre and via Cavour you see today's Romans. Many people living in Rome now have come to the capital from other regions of Italy and they, for the most part, have made their homes in the modern developments on the outskirts of the city. In this area there are some newcomers who have renovated the quaint, rather cramped apartments, but for the most part there are families who have lived here for years. They have "their bar", "their grocery store" and their *vicini di casa* (neighbors), and family is really important, even if it is more dispersed than before. Moods change daily and there is often a temporary falling out , but in an overcrowded city people need a local support system and in this modern suburbia there is a real feeling of community.

On via Nazionale, offices and pensione have for the most part taken over the

apartments above the shops and so there is not a great demand for good food shops. Moving toward the main train station, Termini, multi-ethnic "new Italians" have made their homes here. With their commercial acumen they have improvised temporary street stands where they set out their wares on nothing more than a sheet on the sidewalk.

San Lorenzo has become very fashionable, and many of the older inhabitants, who can still remember the heavy bombing the area received during World War II because of its proximity to the freight train terminus, are rather bemused by the sea-change that has overtaken them. It used to be a working class area but many of the old factory buildings have now been divided into artists' studios and apartments. In a city where central space is at a premium, comparatively inexpensive accommodation has attracted successful people from the world of the arts, and students from the nearby university, La Sapienza. At night the student population gives San Lorenzo a "buzz" and it is very lively with its bars, pizzerias, and trattorias.

In terms of food shopping in the area, there are two high quality grocery stores which shouldn't be missed — Castroni on via Quattro Fontane and Roscioli on via Buonarroti. You can find a variety of delicious fresh pasta in the store Pasta al Uovo and traditional breads in panetteria Venezia Pan. The shop which is the most fun to explore is undoubtedly Enoteca Trimani, the oldest wine shop in the city, which has an incredible selection of Italian wines. For a change from the usual trattorias serving traditional Roman dishes, you can also find trattorias here which specialize in Sicilian and Tuscan dishes.

Agricola Nautia

All the produce in this grocery store comes from the Tevere Farfa Riserva, which fosters and promotes the production of olive oil, cheese, and other foods made by small artisan craftsmen. Many of these producers would have gone out of business without the Riserva's help. As well as this store, there are four other outlets in the city.
VIA DEI CORSI 32, 06 454 248

Castroni

Over the years Castroni has cornered the market in imported food items such as preserves, breakfast cereals, Mexican chili powder, and other gastronomic delights, but they also sell all the best Italian olive oils, balsamic vinegar, tubes of black olive paste, pasta, and rice, as well as nuts, dried fruit, and grains. With few other good food shops in this area, there is a large and grateful clientele. There is a bigger Castroni on via Cola di Rienzo in the Prati area of the city.
VIA QUATTRO FONTANE 37, 06 488 2435

Antica Pescheria 1894 Galuzzi

This small shop supplies fish to many of the best restaurants, and there is a faithful following among staff from the nearby government ministries. Franco goes to the fish auctions in the early hours and the shop is open long before most of the coffee bars. There is a colorful display of fish and Franco will take special orders for seafood such as cape sante (scallops) that are not easy to find in Rome. Franco's wife, Franca, sits at the checkout and soothes him when he gets a little tetchy through lack of sleep.
VIA VENEZIA 26, 06 474 4445

Mercato Quirinale

This little market is under the walls of the Palazzo del Quirinale, the presidential palace in via del Lavatore, and has just a handful of stands selling fruit and vegetables. In the past the market was much larger, but as Romans increasingly choose to shop in supermarkets after work, markets such as this get smaller and smaller. However, there is still a brisk trade here, with tourists from the nearby Trevi Fountain area shopping for an impromptu picnic and residents from the neighborhood picking up a last minute ingredient for the evening meal.

Paci

San Lorenzo, the university area of Rome, has a good selection of trattorias but the scope for shopping is limited. This pastry shop provides all the well-loved cakes to sweeten the pill of an intensive study session, or gladden the hearts of the older inhabitants.

VIA DEI MARSI 35, 06 495 7804

Pasta al Uovo

Time seems to have stood still in this shop. There is a modest display of paglia e fieno (which literally means "straw and hay", but is actually yellow and green fettuccine), and ravioli filled with spinach and ricotta. At the back of the shop a simple pasta machine hums while busily stamping out the pasta. This scene used to be played out in most areas of

Rome fifteen years ago but now it has the charm of novelty. When asked about this, Sergio Caselunghe, who takes pride and quiet satisfaction in his work, replied quite simply that people today prefer to do their shopping in supermarkets. *Che peccato*! (What a pity!).

VIA DEI VOLSCI 97, 06 491 620

Roscioli

Pietro Roscioli's brother owns the famous Roscioli in via Giubbonari so, as you would expect, the quality here is very high. There is a great variety of bread and a tempting salumeria section in this secure citadel of Italian excellence surrounded by the ethnic stores around piazza Vittorio Emanuele II.

VIA BUONARROTI 46/48, 06 446 7146

Venezia Pan

Via Venezia is a short street but it has this good bakery as well as Franco's excellent fish shop, Antica Pescheria 1894 Galuzzi. You'll find wonderful traditional bread and some interesting innovations such as grissini topped with poppy and sesame seeds, along with some general groceries.

VIA VENEZIA 13, 06 488 1324

Enoteca Trimani

Buying wine is rather like buying books — you need to browse in peace with an unobtrusive presence ready to give advice if and when needed. Many wine shops understand this but lack of space makes buying wine a neck-craning experience, with stacked cases of wine making the floor an obstacle course. How satisfying it is to enter the spacious Enoteca Trimani on via Goito. I love this shop and discover new treasures on every visit.

Enoteca Trimani is the oldest wine shop in the city, having supplied Rome with good wine since 1821. It moved to its present home in via Goito in 1876. In the 1980s my Saturday morning treat was to come here to talk to Marco Trimani about wine, discover new producers, and go home with a few bottles to try. Although the shop has been modernized, many of the old features have been carefully preserved. The floor is made of basalt slabs and the great wooden counter has the original Carrara marble top. The fountain, which was used as a wine dispenser, stands in a basin decorated with bunches of grapes. There are large labeled jars that used to hold the wine being cooled by running water and on the wall is a price list dating from 1919.

Despite the changes over the years, it is still a great pleasure to visit the shop to explore the shelves. Wines are arranged by region and I always home in on the Friuli-Veneziana section first. It was here that I first discovered Gravner, Jermann, and Ribolla Gialla. The wines of Campania, such as Falanghina and Greco del Tufo, go very well with the sort of food Romans eat in the summer, and I always enjoy sampling those made by small producers who are new to me. In many wine shops there seem to be wider selections of red wines than whites, but here both are treated fairly. There is a particularly good selection of the great Tuscans, including my favorite Nebbiolo from Piemonte. Although it is anathema to many Italians, Trimani even sells wines from other countries, and there is a section just for "bubbles", and another for beers and spirits. The really important wines are kept in a closed room, so that no tragic accidents with a swinging handbag or walking stick can occur.

In 1991, Trimani expanded to open a wine bar with a separate entrance round the corner in via Cernaia. It is a great place for a civilized drink or a light lunch chosen from a menu which includes a wide selection of salami, French cheeses, soups, and vegetable tarts made with seasonal ingredients, or perhaps oysters or smoked salmon crostini. It can get rather crowded during "happy hour" (which is an innovation in Rome), but the service is always very good. As you would imagine, there is an incredible choice of wines by the glass and having a glass here gives you the opportunity to try a new wine before going next door to buy. All year round except for fall, the new generation of the Trimani family, Carla, Paolo, and Francesca, take it in turns to impart their vast knowledge by holding evening classes geared to different levels of expertise.

Enoteca Trimani, via Goito 20, 06 446 9661
Trimani il Wine Bar, via Cernaia 37b, 06 446 9630

Penne Arrabbiata

Pasta with tomato and chile sauce

This spicy dish is quick to prepare and full of flavor. Remember not to add the pasta to the boiling water until the sauce is ready. As Italians say, the sauce waits for the pasta, the pasta never waits for the sauce.

SERVES 4
PREPARATION TIME: 20 MINUTES
COOKING TIME: 30 MINUTES

½ red bell pepper, seeded and
    thickly sliced
1 dried chile pepper
1 garlic clove, finely chopped
500g/1lb 2oz penne pasta
2tbsp grated Parmesan cheese
handful of chopped flat-leaf
    parsley to garnish

TOMATO SAUCE:
2tbsp extra virgin olive oil
1 small onion, finely chopped
2 garlic cloves, finely chopped
800g/28oz canned peeled
    Italian plum tomatoes
salt and freshly ground
    black pepper
2tbsp basil leaves, roughly
    torn

To make the tomato sauce, heat half the oil in a skillet and cook the onion and garlic over a low heat until soft. Add the tomatoes and cook over a high heat until most of the juice has evaporated. Put through a food mill or sieve, season with salt and pepper to taste, and add the basil.

Heat the remaining oil in a saucepan, add the sliced pepper and fry for 5 minutes until soft. Then add the chile pepper and garlic and fry until the garlic begins to change color before stirring in the tomato sauce and warming through.

Cook the penne according to the instructions on the pack until al dente. Drain and toss with the sauce. Garnish with the parsley and sprinkle with the grated Parmesan cheese and serve at once.

Involtini di Melanzane

Eggplant (aubergine) rolls

Although traditionally the eggplant slices are fried, they can be grilled to make a lighter starter, or the quantities increased to make a vegetarian main dish.

SERVES 4
PREPARATION TIME: 50–60 MINUTES
COOKING TIME: 15 MINUTES

500g/1lb 2oz eggplants
    (aubergines)
250g/½lb fresh mozzarella
fresh basil leaves
2tbsp olive oil for frying
2tbsp freshly grated Parmesan

salt and freshly ground
    black pepper
1 cup freshly-made tomato
    sauce (see Penne Arrabbiata
    recipe)

Cut off the rounded tips of the eggplants (aubergines) and discard them. Then cut the eggplants (aubergines) into thin slices, lengthwise. Sprinkle the slices with coarse salt and leave for 30 minutes until they 'purge' their bitter juices.

While you are waiting for the eggplants, prepare the tomato sauce according to the penne arrabbiata recipe.

Cut the mozzarella into thick slices and divide each slice into batons, allowing one baton for each eggplant slice. Then rinse the salt off the eggplant slices and dry each one very thoroughly.

Heat the oil in a skillet and fry the slices of eggplant in batches until they are golden brown on each side. Allow the excess oil to drain off on paper towels.

Lightly oil an ovenproof serving dish that will contain all the rolls in one layer. Roll each eggplant slice round a baton of mozzarella and a basil leaf, and arrange seam side down in the oven dish. Spoon a little tomato sauce over the rolls but do not mask the individual rolls completely. Sprinkle a little Parmesan over the top and bake at 180°C/350°F for 15 minutes in a preheated oven.

Restaurants in Piazza Venezia, Via Nazionale & San Lorenzo

Il Dito e la Luna

Claudio's was one of the first trattorias to bring a fresh look to the eating-out scene in San Lorenzo. He is Sicilian and most of the dishes show his origins. There is pasta alla Norma (pasta with a tomato and eggplant sauce), couscous with fish and vegetables, which is a specialty from Trapani, on the west coast of Sicily, and delicious swordfish cooked with olives, capers, and tomatoes. The desserts are interesting, with a good tortino di cioccolato (chocolate "pie", without pastry), and a selection of Sicilian cheeses.

Via dei Sabelli 51, 06 494 0726

Al Chianti

For many years this restaurant has given Porta Pia a Tuscan flavor. To start with there are crostini, followed by zuppa di farro (soup made with spelt, an old variety of wheat that is becoming popular), or the ribollita, a thick vegetable soup. In spring, there is pasta with fresh peas, and in the cold months pappardelle al lepre (pappardelle with a rich hare sauce). The castagnaccio (chestnut and rosemary cake) has many enthusiastic takers.

Via Ancona 17, 06 4425 0242

Da Marcello

Many classic Roman dishes are carefully prepared in this friendly, traditional trattoria. Recommended pasta sauces include alla coda (with oxtail sauce), Matriciana, and gricia (with garlic and bacon). Many Romans come here to San Lorenzo to enjoy the cacio e pepe or the traditional tasty sausage and beans.

Via dei Campani 12, 06 446 3311

Formula 1

This well-established pizzeria is always full of young people wanting to eat well at a very reasonable price. The service is quick and there are over one hundred pizza toppings to choose from. The fried Roman favorites are good and there is a tasty vegetable antipasto.
VIA DEGLI EQUI 13, 06 445 3866

Pommidoro

Anna and Aldo have been running this popular trattoria for many years, helped by their daughters. The grandchildren are often visible and you get the feeling of being part of warm family life. Anna reigns in the kitchen and Aldo grills tasty meat on the open fire. A good carbonara is not easy to find, but you can order it here with confidence. Their pasta with porcini mushrooms is not to be missed and game is occasionally available in the fall and winter. In warm weather tables are put out in the piazza and people sit with a carafe of wine, watching the world go by.
PIAZZA DEI SANNITI 44, 06 445 2692

Vinarium

Originally a wine bar but now a dinner-only restaurant, Vinarium still has a great wine list. Added to this is an imaginative menu where traditional dishes are given a new twist. The classic melanzane alla parmigiana is lighter and more delicate without tomato sauce, and the Ligurian *cucina povera* combination of pesto, green beans, and potatoes transforms a dish of wholewheat lasagne. Among the desserts, the filling of the Neapolitan pastiera (tart with wheat grains, ricotta, and candied fruits) is particularly successful.
VIA DEI VOLSCI 107, 06 446 2110

Tram Tram

Don't let the rather unpromising setting with tramlines running down the middle of a shabby, narrow street put you off. The signora is Pugliese and her fave e cicoria (fava beans anointed with good olive oil) is exceptional. Although the menu contains the classic ear-shaped pasta from Puglia, orecchiette, served with broccoli, clams add a new dimension. The linguine with calamari and pesto has echoes of Liguria.
VIA DEI RETI 44/46, 06 490 416

Zuppa del Venerdi Santo

Good Friday soup

Good Friday is not a public holiday in Italy and even twenty years ago I remember being really surprised to see people in restaurants tucking into their steaks and chicken. However, in the past, when Friday was still a "lean" or meat-free day, fish soup was traditional Good Friday fare for the Romans.

SERVES 4
PREPARATION TIME: 30 MINUTES
COOKING TIME: 1 HOUR

1kg/2¼lb shrimp in their shells
4tbsp olive oil
2 whole salted anchovies or 6 fillets, chopped
handful of chopped parsley
4 garlic cloves, minced
200g/7oz peeled Italian tomatoes, puréed or put through a sieve

1 chile pepper
salt
4 thick slices of bread

STOCK:
1 celery stick, chopped
1 carrot, chopped
1 small onion, diced
1 bay leaf

Clean the shellfish and remove the heads and shells but do not throw them away. Cut the shrimp into thin strips.

To make the stock, put the shrimp heads and shells into a very large saucepan, then add the celery, carrot, onion, bay leaf, and enough water to cover. Simmer for 20 minutes. Strain the stock and measure 2 liters/3½ pints/8 cups. If necessary, either boil the stock further until reduced, or dilute it to obtain the required amount.

Heat the oil in a large saucepan set over a medium heat, add the finely chopped anchovies, parsley and garlic, and fry until the garlic begins to color. Add the tomatoes and shrimp stock and simmer for 20 minutes.

Add the shrimp strips to the soup and simmer gently for a further 5 minutes before adding the chile pepper and a little salt.

Toast the bread and put a slice at the bottom of each warm soup bowl before pouring on the hot soup. Serve immediately.

Abbacchio alla Cacciatora

Lamb with white wine vinegar, and rosemary

There are many, many variations of cacciatora recipes. This one works very well with lamb. *Abbacchio* is very young lamb; if you are only able to buy older lamb, use a different cut, such as half a shoulder. Italians always prefer to cook meat on the bone because it adds extra flavor to the finished dish.

SERVES 4
PREPARATION TIME: 10 MINUTES
COOKING TIME: 1 HOUR

1kg/2¼lb leg of lamb on the bone, chopped into pieces weighing about 45g/1¾oz
salt and freshly ground black pepper
3tbsp olive oil
3 garlic cloves, finely chopped
3tbsp fresh rosemary needles, chopped

1tbsp all-purpose (plain) flour
225ml/8fl oz/1 cup white wine vinegar
225ml/8fl oz/1 cup water
225ml/8fl oz/1 cup dry white wine or water

Season the lamb with salt and pepper. Heat the oil in a large, heavy, deep skillet or a saucepan set over a medium heat and quickly brown the lamb on all sides. Sprinkle with the garlic and rosemary and stir for 5 minutes. Sprinkle the flour over the lamb, stir well then pour in the vinegar — stand back a little in case it splutters over you. Stir for a few minutes, then add the water and cover. Simmer, stirring occasionally, for 35 minutes for young lamb, or longer for older lamb, until the meat is tender and falling off the bone. The sauce should be thick and dark; add a tablespoonful or two of water or white wine if it becomes too dry.

Remove the lamb with a slotted spoon. Pass the sauce through a sieve, taste and adjust the seasoning if necessary, then pour into a clean saucepan to warm through. Serve the lamb on warm plates with the sauce poured over.

Landmarks

This area of the city runs from the Capitoline Hill, past the imposing, white marble monument to Vittorio Emanuele II and up to the Terme di Diocleziano baths via the faded grandeur of via Nazionale. Beyond is the university area of the city, San Lorenzo. On route you'll pass fountains and ancient Rome's shopping mall, as well as an impressive column more than one hundred and thirty feet high.

Capitolium

In ancient Rome, the Capitol was the city's citadel and all the most important ceremonies took place there. A winding path led up from the Forum and at the top there was a temple to Jupiter, and an early temple to Juno. When Rome was under attack from the Gauls in 390 BC the enemy stealthily climbed up to try to take the Capitol by night. Juno's sacred geese gave the alarm with their honking and the Roman soldiers managed to repel the attack and so save Rome. A new temple to Juno was subsequently built.

The hill remained important to Rome in the following centuries. In 1341 Petrarch was presented with the poet's laurel wreath on the Capitol and some forty years later, when the Black Death swept Rome, the Aracoeli church was built there. There are one hundred and twenty-two steep, narrow steps leading up to the church, in great contrast to the wide, graceful staircase, the Cordonata, designed by Michelangelo in 1536 (below). This leads up to piazza Campidoglio, with its paved courtyard and magnificent equestrian statue of Marcus Aurelius, which was erected in honor of the Holy Roman Emperor Charles V on his visit to Rome. Today it is the home of Rome's town hall and is the setting for civil marriage ceremonies.

Colonna Traiana

Trajan's Column is one of the oldest and best preserved ancient monuments in Rome. It was built in AD 113 and there are more than one hundred bas-relief scenes depicting Trajan's war with the Dacians. Two thousand five hundred figures decorate twenty five great blocks of marble, each one several feet wide. Trajan's ashes are under the column but the statue of the emperor that used to be on the top was replaced by one of St. Peter in 1587.

Mercati Traianei

Trajan's markets were built at the beginning of the first century AD and included a covered shopping arcade as well as more than one hundred and fifty stores — in essence, an ancient Roman shopping mall. Today the different buildings in the complex contain exhibits on ancient Roman history and art.

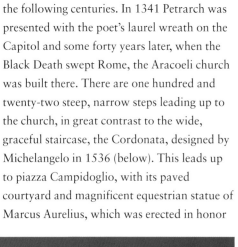

Pages 114–15: the intricate bas-relief on Trajan's Column shows episodes from Trajan's campaigns against the Dacians as well as the everyday lives of the soldiers.

Piazza della Repubblica

At the eastern end of via Nazionale is piazza della Repubblica, which was rebuilt in 1901 and renamed in honor of the new Italian state. Many Romans still use the old name, piazza Esedra, from the exedra of Diocletian's great bath complex (an exedra being a semicircular recess, headed by a half-dome which is often set into a building's facade). When the piazza was first built, there were fashionable shops in the colonnaded arches around it, but as the area declined, they were taken over by offices. Today a luxury hotel is helping to restore some of the piazza's former elegance.

Terme di Diocleziano

The Terme di Diocleziano baths complex was the largest to be built in Rome and could accommodate 3,000 people. It covered a large area, and traces of the baths can be seen in the nearby Church of Santa Maria degli Angeli e dei Martiri, which was built in the remains of the baths. The Museo Nazionale Romano (below) is in these ruins and has important finds from republican and imperial Rome, as well as the extensive Ludovisi collection. The elaborate central Fontana delle Naiadi was designed by the Sicilian sculptor, Rutelli.

Via Nazionale

Via Nazionale is the main commercial street in modern Rome. It is rather noisy and dusty, with an ever increasing amount of traffic. To the side is via delle Quattro Fontane, famous for the four corner fountains depicting the River Tiber with the she-wolf, the River Aniene, and fountains to Juno (symbolizing strength) and Diana (symbolizing fidelity). The small Church of San Carlo, from 1667, was probably one of Borromini's last works.

Colosseo & Esquilino

The twin attractions of the Colosseum and the Roman Forum draw visitors to this area in the thousands, and you'll pay a premium for a table with a two-thousand-year-old view. Those in the know seek out the wonderful fish restaurants, and the fun and friendly Esquilino market, where sacks of Mexican black beans, Indian soy (soya), bright yellow polenta, and pistachio nuts are squashed together. Via Merulana has the bonus of the incredible bread and cake shop Panella, as well as the divine mozzarella from La Mazzarona, sent to the store daily from Caserta in Campania.

Colosseo & Esquilino

To many people Rome *is* the Colosseum. This feeling is summed up in the poet Lord Byron's famous translation of the words of the Venerable Bede, a religious scholar who lived in Britain in 700 AD. "While stands the Colosseum, Rome shall stand; When falls the Colosseum, Rome shall fall; And when Rome falls — the world."

I find it fascinating to see what aspects of Rome appeal to visitors. Some of them love to wander round the ancient ruins and spend hours gazing at the Colosseum and Forum, while others come for the churches. Many of those come to the churches, not through religious fervor, but for the paintings and sculptures contained within. All of the churches in this chapter are packed with art treasures, too rich a feast for a short visit. Those who come for the food and wine have a more relaxing time.

In this area the main food focus is the Esquilino market. This used to be in the large piazza Vittorio Emanuele with the stands grouped round the central garden, but a few years ago it was moved to a large building that was formerly a military barracks. When the market first opened in this setting I found it too pristine and cold. Now the market traders have rubbed down some of the initial gloss and you can have fun shopping and exploring.

The Esquilino market pulses with life. Objectively it is not an area of great beauty but I love coming here. There are four main entrances — in via Principe Amadeo, via Ricasoli, via Turati, and via Lamarmora. When you enter the market by one gate you seem to be in a mini Chinatown and when you leave by another, it's like Little India. It is a real labyrinth and I always seem to get lost as I wander round the maze of stands. There are exotic food emporiums and inexpensive eating places framing the market building and inside it feels like the tower of Babel with an incredible mix of nationalities and languages.

There must be twenty stands selling meat and at least fifteen stands selling fruit and vegetables, with some of the vendors offering vegetables I have not yet managed to identify. The endless rows of meat stands cater to all religious dietary laws. In the center a large courtyard houses the fish stands and one of the market traders, who has a penchant for classical literature, has a banner declaring "*Et in Arcadia ego*". I have always imagined a more sylvan Arcadia and some of the displayed fish seem too malevolent to belong to any idyll.

The market is always busy yet there is a pervading mood of good humor. Years ago Indian spices and herbs weren't available in Rome but today there is a large Indian presence here and I spend many happy mornings discussing Indian regional diversity as I shop for fresh coriander and green chiles. There is no hint of racial tension here and the young men beam when they learn you have visited their country and understand their food. Ethiopia and Eritrea are well represented in produce and eating places, and on my last visit I spotted a new Romanian foods stand.

Although the Esquilino has a vast amount of ethnic foods it is also great for Italian produce. In other markets in Rome there are fewer stands and therefore less choice, but here you will find everything you need for every regional Italian dish you can think of and you can choose between ripe and unripe fruit. Every shape and size of seasonal vegetable is on offer and the green leaves and herbs are the freshest to be found. The market also sells bread, pizza, cheeses, hams, and sacks of rice, pulses, and cereals. If you love food it's certain that you will love this market, even if you have nowhere in Rome to cook.

In this part of Rome you can pay a visit to another Roman institution, Panella. This superlative bakery is more than a century old and attracts people from all over the city. Its original window displays of Nativity and Easter scenes made entirely out of bread are legendary, and the in-store coffee bar revives even the weariest shoppers.

You can shop *and* eat well in this district. For the freshest fish Il Tempio di Iside is a great option, and for classic fresh pasta dishes you'll have to elbow the regulars out of the way for a table at Trattoria Monti. The unchanging menu keeps locals coming back for their favorite dishes.

Page 120: the Foro Romano (seen here with the Colosseum in the background), was the religious, commercial, economic, and political heart of Republican Rome. Its buildings and ruins span almost a thousand years of history.

Mercato Esquilino

The multi-ethnic market that used to be housed in piazza Vittorio Emanuele was moved a few years ago to a disused barracks nearer Termini train station. It is now a covered market with several entrances. This is the cheapest market in Rome and the choice can be bewildering. You are likely to see vegetables you never knew existed, great displays of spices from India, Africa, and the Mid-East, and rows of stands selling meat, including halal. There is an entire hall devoted to fish offering a wide choice at fair prices, but you need to have a knowledgeable eye where fresh fish is concerned, and be particularly careful when buying shellfish. In another hall you'll find exotic fruits and herbs like cilantro (coriander) and dill.

Via Principe Amedeo

L'Antica Cornetteria

This pastry shop is a good place to satisfy hunger pangs after a late party or to gladden the heart of the *nottambuli* (night-owls). It sells great cornetti (croissants) and breakfast pastries at antisocial hours, and will make cakes and finger food for birthdays and other special occasions. The store claims to open at 5am, but when asked at what hour they close, the answer was "Never"!

Via Labicana 78, 06 7045 4084

Antico Forno Romano la Piastra dal 1895

In this bakery you'll find many regional specialties, all of them good, including pane Altamura, the eponymous bread made with bran that is typical of the small town of Altamura between Puglia and Basilicata. They also sell great round loaves of pane casasreccio (coarse bread), which makes good bruschetta. When people used to make their own bread at home once a week, potato was incorporated into the dough to keep it from going stale too quickly.

Via Labicana 12/14, 06 7049 6438

L'Arte di Sicilia

The pastry chef is Sicilian and he makes all of the great Sicilan dolci (desserts): lovely, pale green cassate (Sicilian ice-cream cake), sinful canoli (deep-fried pastries filled with ricotta and candied fruits), and torta paradiso (a light type of pound cake). Many of the ingredients are brought from Sicily, including pistachio nuts from Bronte.

Via dei Valeri 13, 06 7049 7518

Bottega Liberati

Many of Rome's top restaurants are proud to mention on their websites that they buy their meat from this family-run butcher. As well as the highest quality meat, including delicious prosciutto crudo, they also sell cheeses and other gastronomic specialties and give you the benefit of their expertise.

Via Flavio Stilicone 278/282,
06 7154 4153

La Mazzonara

Although other latticini (soft cheeses) are sold in this cheese shop, the specialty is very, very good mozzarella, which is sent here daily from near Caserta. You can order it in different shapes and sizes, although the larger ones are believed to have the most flavor. Other cheeses include ricotta, smoked scamorze (a soft, distinctively shaped cow's milk cheese), and giuncata. This last is traditionally made by pressing the lightly salted, soft fresh cheese into small rush baskets, although nowadays the producers tend to use plastic, which is more hygienic but less appealing. The name of the cheese is derived from the Italian word *giunco*, which means "rush".

Via Merulana 76A, 06 7045 3464

Panella

This incredible shop was started by Augusto Panella at the beginning of the last century and today it is a Roman institution. The tagline to the shop's name, L'Arte del Pane, truly reflects their attitude toward bread. At Christmas the window display of the nativity scene, with every character, animal, and building made of bread, is worth a detour. All through the year every special event is chronicled in bread. At Carnevale, the period before Lent, the traditional frappe (deep-fried strips of sweet pastry) are gaily colored like the paper confetti thrown in the streets. At Easter they make individual bread chickens, complete with attached hard-cooked (hard-boiled) egg.

Maria Grazia Panella manages to combine authenticity with innovation. The range of bread is incredible and the pizza and pastry sections attract long queues on Sunday mornings. In fact it's difficult to find the shop quiet. People come here not just to buy bread but also to stock up on fresh pasta, cookies, and irresistible fruit tarts. One area sells specialty flours and grains, dried herbs and spices, and some imported goodies. There is a small bar where, jostled by the crowd of shoppers, you can stand and have a reviving coffee or aperitivo, and sample the delights on sale. This store is expensive but it is a unique experience — a feast for the eyes as well as the stomach.

Via Merulana 54, 06 487 2344

Pages 124–5: the covered Esquilino market is where Romans stock up on everything from fruit and vegetables, through meat and fish, to exotic spices.

Spigola in Acqua Pazza

Sea bass in "mad water"

This simple fish recipe has gained popularity in Rome although originally it was a fishermen's dish. They would set out to sea equipped with olive oil, garlic, chile pepper, and a few tomatoes. The least valuable fish that were caught would be cooked straight from the sea on the hot rims of acetylene lamps, using sea water "maddened" by the garlic and chile pepper. Only attempt to make this recipe with really fresh fish, and remember that the small tomatoes should make orange flecks in the transparent sauce, not an opaque mask. If you prefer fish fillets, get some fish bones and boil them in plain water for 15 minutes to make fish stock to use instead of boiling water.

SERVES 4
PREPARATION TIME: 10 MINUTES
COOKING TIME: 4–5 MINUTES

4tbsp extra virgin olive oil
2 garlic cloves, chopped
1 dried chile pepper, crushed
2 sea bass, cleaned and scaled
salt and freshly ground
   black pepper
450ml/16fl oz/2 cups boiling
   water
8 cherry tomatoes
1tbsp chopped fresh parsley

Choose a large skillet, big enough to hold both fish in one layer. Add the oil and set over a medium heat, then add the garlic, chile, and fish. Season the fish and after 2–3 minutes pour in the boiling water. Cut a slit in the skin of each tomato, add to the pan, and, using the back of a wooden spoon, squash them against the sides. Sprinkle in the parsley, cover and cook gently for approximately 20 minutes until the thickest part of the fish flakes when tested with the point of a sharp knife.

Carefully remove the fish from the pan to avoid breaking them and lift the flesh from the bones. The fillets should come away from the bones without too much difficulty. Serve the fillets with spoonfuls of cooking liquid, leaving the tomato skins in the pan.

Tagliato di Manzo

Sliced thick beef steak with garlic and rosemary

This used to be found only in Tuscany, but as good beef is now available in Rome, restaurants have started serving it. At home it is difficult to cook it to please a lot of people, so I tend to do it for two. I usually serve it with strips of roasted red bell peppers and red onion.

SERVES 2
PREPARATION TIME: 10 MINUTES, PLUS 1 HOUR MINIMUM
MARINATING
COOKING TIME: 5–10 MINUTES

1 rib (entrecôte) steak, about
   400g/14oz and 4cm/1¾ inches
   thick
2 garlic cloves, coarsely
   chopped
1tbsp fresh rosemary, chopped
2tbsp extra virgin olive oil,
   plus extra for brushing
salt and freshly ground
   black pepper

Put the steak in a non-metallic container — it should be large enough to hold the meat snugly — and sprinkle with the garlic, rosemary, and olive oil. Leave to marinate at room temperature for at least 1 hour, turning the meat occasionally. Reserve the marinade.

Preheat the oven to 240°C/475°F/gas mark 9. Brush a heavy ridged pan or a heavy skillet with oil and set it over a high heat. Add the beef and quickly sear it on both sides. Immediately remove the meat from the pan and cut it into thick diagonal slices across the grain.

Arrange the slices of meat flat on two ovenproof plates, pouring some of the oil marinade over the top. Cook in the oven for approximately 3 minutes for rare, 6 minutes for medium, or 8 minutes for well done, depending on how you like your beef cooked. As these timings are approximate, it is best to keep a close eye on the beef as it is cooking, to make sure it is cooked the way you like it.

Domenico dal 1968

The family which owns this trattoria originally came from Rieti, near Amatrice, a town known for its good food. There's a choice of meat or fish and the pasta e ceci and the fried vegetables are excellent.

Via Satirico 21, 06 7049 4602

Gioco Liscio

This is another real family trattoria which is run with love and care — I come here to eat the fantastic zuppa di lenticchie (lentil soup). Other dishes include gnocchi alla Matriciana and baked cod with potatoes.

Via Voghera 10, 06 701 2811

Luzzi

Luzzi is situated very close to the Church of San Clemente in the pleasant valley between the Esquiline and Oppio hills. They serve thin, crispy pizza and Roman specialties, among other things, and the prices are hard to beat. Choose from pasta all'arrabbiata (with a tomato and chile sauce), lasagne al forno, tortellini ai funghi porcini, and a lamb dish, abbacchio al forno.

Via San Giovanni in Laterano 88, 06 709 6332

Ottavio

This is a good, serious fish restaurant with an interesting menu; spigola (sea bass) and orata (bream) are cooked under a salt crust or in guazzetto (steamed with herbs to make a clear sauce). The primi piatti are all good, especially linguine with moscardini (tiny octopus). Like most fish restaurants, it is closed on Monday.

Via Santa Croce in Gerusalemme 9, 06 702 0520

Ponte della Ranocchia

The rather spartan wooden chairs on the wide sidewalk outside the trattoria act as a signal that the inside is simple, almost austere. People come here every day for the food, rather than for the atmosphere. The menu is short but interesting, with unusual combinations. The penne with sun-dried tomatoes and octopus is delicious, as is the rich specialty, fettuccine with goose prosciutto and Cornish game hen (guinea fowl) sauce. With a fine selection of desserts and a fair wine list, it all adds up to good value.

Circonvillazione Appia 29, 06 785 6712

Ristorante Papagio'

Around the Celio hill there are a few streets that have a village atmosphere, with the locals still shopping for food every morning in the small street market. This charming restaurant has a good menu, with meat, fish and seafood, risotto, and excellent pasta dishes which make use of traditional ingredients in an original way. The small wine list is carefully compiled.

Via Capo d'Africa 26, 06 7726 2953

Grazie a Dio è Venerdi

One of the oldest ovens in this historic area is in use in this pizzeria. It used to be a bread oven but today it is used for baking at least fifty different types of thin, crispy pizza. There are other dishes, but this is what most people come here for.

Via dei Capacci 1, 06 488 2585

Trattoria Monti

This is a classic restaurant run by a family from le Marche area of Italy. The menu, containing the classic fresh pasta for which that region is known, changes little, which is just as well, because most of the customers are regulars who come here to enjoy their favorites. Many of Franca's traditional recipes have been almost forgotten elsewhere. Some of the treats include a delicate zucchini sformati (courgette), delicious tortelli (which are large stuffed pasta shapes), and pasta with a robust duck sauce.

VIA SAN VITO 13, 06 446 6573

Pages 130–1: the multi-ethnic Esquilino market sells grains, pulses, beans, and flours, many of which can't be found anywhere else in the city.

Il Tempio di Iside

Il Tempio, on the corner of piazza Iside, is a great fish restaurant. Their fish "sa il mare", or "knows the sea" as the Italians say, meaning that it is very fresh. The prices are fair considering the restaurant's location so close to the Colosseum and the atmosphere is calm and relaxed. The menu is a mixture of the traditional and the innovative, but the latter are never too elaborate, with dishes such as swordfish agnoletti (small stuffed pasta, similar to ravioli) with a bell pepper sauce, and simple acqua pazza (fish cooked in water flavored with chiles, garlic, and tomatoes), which only works with fish fresh from the sea. As you would expect from a fish restaurant, it is closed on Monday.

VIA VERRI 11, 06 700 4741

Puntarelle in Salsa di Alici
Asparagus chicory with anchovy sauce

For this dish you need the wild asparagus family chicory. It is one of Rome's favorite ingredients for salads, and in the markets the older market traders sit preparing vast curly mounds. The dressing, which is great with other wild-leaf salads too, can also be used as a dip for crudités.

SERVES 4
PREPARATION TIME: 15 MINUTES

500g/1lb 2oz washed, trimmed puntarelle, or other wild salad leaves
1 garlic clove, chopped
4 anchovy fillets, chopped

2tbsp white wine vinegar
4tbsp extra virgin olive oil
salt and freshly ground black pepper

Cut the puntarelle stalks lengthwise into thin strips and put them in a bowl of cold water until they curl — usually at least 30 minutes.

Although traditionally the anchovy sauce is made by pounding in a pestle and mortar, a small blender or food processor can be used.

Put in the garlic, anchovies, and vinegar and process briefly. With the motor running, slowly pour in the oil. Add salt and pepper to taste. You will need pepper but the anchovies will probably provide enough salt.

Drain the puntarelle and pat dry with paper towels, if necessary. Drizzle the dressing over the salad and serve.

Pizza Rustica

Classic pizza dough

Although deep pizzas have their fans, my love is reserved for the thin, crisp sheets of takeout pizza (pizza rustica), that are baked in great trays and sold by the slice. When I am near one of my favorite pizza shops I can't resist going in. I stand in line with the workmen, students, and elegant Romans waiting for my choice-of-the-day, straight from the oven. This dough can either be rolled out to fill large rectangular trays or divided into balls to make round pizzas. Romans love the potato and rosemary topping, though others like arugula (rocket), pine nuts, and crumbled ricotta are also popular.

SERVES 4

PREPARATION TIME: 1 HOUR 20 MINUTES, INCLUDING TIME FOR THE DOUGH TO RISE

COOKING TIME: 30 MINUTES

25g/1oz fresh yeast*
275ml/½ pint/1¼ cups warm
   water
1tbsp olive oil
500g/1lb 2oz/4½ cups white
   all-purpose flour
1tsp salt

POTATO AND ROSEMARY
   TOPPING (OPTIONAL):
salt and freshly ground black
   pepper
400g/14oz small potatoes,
   unpeeled
1tbsp finely chopped fresh
   rosemary needles
1tbsp olive oil

Cream the yeast with a little of the warm water, then add the oil.

Sift the flour in a bowl or a food processor and stir in the salt. Make a well in the center and pour in the yeast mixture. Slowly pour in the remaining warm water while drawing in the flour, using your fingers, to make a stiff, but not sticky, dough. Knead the dough until it is smooth and elastic; this will take 10–15 minutes if kneading by hand, or 3–5 minutes if using a food processor or table-top mixer.

Cover the dough with plastic wrap or, better still, form it into a ball and put it into a large, oiled plastic bag. Leave to rise in a warm place for about 1 hour until it has doubled in volume.

If you wish to make the potato and rosemary topping, start by bringing a large pan of lightly salted water to the boil. Add the

potatoes, still in their skins, and boil for 10–15 minutes, or until a knife can be easily inserted into the side of a potato. Drain, then leave until cool enough to handle. The skins should slide off easily now, but if not, just peel them and then cut into thin slices.

Preheat the oven to 240°C/475°F/gas mark 9. Put the dough onto a floured counter and knead briefly before rolling out to 1cm/½ inch thick.

Arrange the potato slices slightly overlapping on the pizza base. Sprinkle with the rosemary and season with salt and plenty of black pepper. Drizzle with the olive oil and bake for 15 minutes.

* If fresh yeast is not available, use 1 tablespoon instant dried yeast and stir it into the flour.

Landmarks

In this, the heart of ancient Rome, you'll find centuries-old monuments as well as several beautiful churches. The seemingly indestructible Colosseum dominates the landscape and the sight of it never fails to take the breath away. The buildings of the Roman Forum span a thousand years of history, although its lone columns, fallen masonry, and statues give few clues to its former grandeur and significance.

Colosseo

The Colosseum (below left and pages 138–9) is the largest surviving ancient Roman structure in the world and completely dominates this area of Rome. It was built by Emperor Vespasian in AD 72 on the site of the lake that used to be part of Nero's great palace, the Domus Aurea, and in its day could hold more than 50,000 people. Spectators flocked here to witness barbaric gladiatorial games, executions, individual combats between men and wild animals, and, most spectacularly of all, naumachia. During this spectacle, the amphitheater was deliberately flooded so that slaves and criminals on small galleys could re-enact naval battles.

Foro Romano

The Forum (top right) was the political, commercial, religious, and economic hub of the city during republican times. It was the home of the law courts and banking and was the venue for religious ceremonies and important funerals, among other things. As the city's main meeting place it fulfilled the same purpose as the piazza does in twenty-first century Italy.

Palatino

The Palatine hill provides one of the most pleasant walks in this area, high above the snarling traffic. During the days of the republic, the patricians had their houses here; in fact Octavius was born here. When he became Emperor Augustus he asked the Senate for a modest house on the Palatine hill, and it was later emperors, such as Tiberius and Caligula, who built palaces and turned it into an imperial hill.

San Clemente

This is one of Rome's oldest basilicas and was named after San Clemente, a Pope who was martyred in the first century. The building has been added to many times over the centuries and was used at different times as a residence, a mint, and a warehouse, as well as a place of worship. For many visitors the highlight is the golden twelfth-century mosaic in the apse of the upper basilica that depicts the Crucifixion.

San Giovanni in Laterano

San Giovanni was built in the sixteenth century but incorporates the remaining wings of the Lateran Palace, which housed the Popes until 1309. Today, you can see the original cloisters with their twisted columns (right and top left), and the Pope's private chapel. The Scala Santa is believed to be the flight of twenty steps that Jesus climbed on his way to be tried in Pontius Pilate's house. The steps are covered with boards so that no foot touches them, and even pilgrims have to climb the holy stairs on their knees.

San Pietro in Vincoli

The church was built by Pope Leo I in the fifth century AD to house the chains believed to be those which were used to fetter St. Peter before his death. They were returned to Rome from Constantinople. Today visitors come to look at Michelangelo's great statue of Moses. The horns on Moses's head might seem a little puzzling: apparently when the Old Testament was translated from Hebrew, what should have been beams of light became horns.

Pages 134–5: this part of the Church of San Clemente is undergound, and was used as a temple to worship the Persian god Mithras.

Testaccio

Testaccio is south of the Palatine hill and the Colosseum, and is a traditional working-class *quartiere* where the city's slaughterhouses once stood. The offcuts which the workers received as part of their pay led to quintessential Roman dishes like oxtail stew, coda alla vaccinara, which are still served in some restaurants here. The historic and fashionable restaurant Checchino dal 1887 is an added draw for food lovers, although the principal attraction for many is the food market, which is the best, if not the most beautiful, that the city has to offer.

Testaccio

Testaccio might not have the glory and grandeur of other parts of Rome but it is vibrantly alive and, for me, is the gastronomic heart of Rome. In this area food is a serious business. The market in the central square consists of stands crowded together higgledy-piggledy — a photographer's nightmare with its mix of neon, electric, and limited daylight.

The stands pulse with good humor. Every sneeze is greeted with a "Salute" and there is always time to joke, commiserate, or exchange a recipe. All around cars hoot, motorbikes snarl, and distant sirens wail, but inside the market everyone is absorbed in the rhythm of shopping for food. The fish stands display their glistening catch with panache, and

passers-by are exhorted to buy with the fervor of evangelist preachers. The two stands nearest to the corner pharmacy have the best selection. At this end of the market Massimo sells excellent bread and Valentino has a good herb selection, as well as exotic fruit. The two rows of butchers take great pride in their work, patiently trimming off fat, grinding the

chosen pieces of meat, and smiling as they satisfy the often unreasonable demands of their customers. Appropriate herbs are selected and tucked in with the meat as the butchers move on to discuss the rival merits of the Roma and Lazio soccer players. At the fruit and vegetable stands bags are handed out so that customers can hand-pick what they want, and even potatoes are subject to the keenest scrutiny.

Testaccio was originally developed in the early twentieth century to house the workers who were needed for the new industries in Ostiense and the modern slaughterhouse, the Mattatoio, which opened in 1890. Sadly the tall apartment blocks have little to recommend them, because every attempt to build the città-giardino (garden city) proved too expensive.

In piazza Bernini, in front of the tenth-century church, Santa Saba, there is a delightful little market and several good food shops. The older relatives of the market traders sit shucking peas, cleaning artichokes, and slicing the *catalogno* (a type of chicory) to transform it into gleaming piles of *puntarelle* (asparagus chicory). On cold winter mornings, they break up the packing boxes and use the pieces to light impromptu fires to keep themselves warm. Here you get the feeling that you are in a village rather than a city, with the slower pace of life. The little houses around the square, each with its own small garden, are very appealing, and on the seats in the central garden grandfathers can usually be seen discussing food or soccer, or reading the daily paper while supervising babies in prams. Cats bask in the sun, and around lunchtime a little crowd forms outside the small church school, waiting for the children to come home for their midday meal.

Traditionally Roman cooking is simple and direct with the strong flavors so beloved by the ancient Romans. There has been no elegant court life to inspire chefs to great imaginative feats, and even in the past when some of the Popes were overinterested in food, it was because they were gluttons rather than gourmets. A few years ago a cultured Neapolitan Prince I met dismissed Rome (and by implication its cuisine) as nothing but a city of priests and politicians. I retaliated by launching into a paean of praise for Roman cuisine. My argument would have been less convincing if I had got on to the subject of Testaccio's tradition of using variety meats (offcuts) — this type of meat is far less appealing to lighter, modern tastes.

When Rome became the capital of a unified Italy laborers were brought in from the surrounding countryside to work in the large, modern slaughterhouse. Part of their wages consisted of the sections of the animal that had no commercial value — the fifth quarter, known in Italian as the *quinto quarto*. The slaughterhouse workers took this "prize" to the local wineshops, which in those days served simple food, and the cooks invented ways to make the offcuts of intestines, heads, feet, and even tails appetizing. And so the legendary dishes *pajata* (made with the intestine of ox or veal), and *coda alla vaccinara* (oxtail stew) came to be an intrinsic part of Roman cooking. Today connoisseurs brave Rome's chaotic rush hour traffic to dine on these dishes in Testaccio restaurants, in the neighborhood where they were first created.

143

Shops in Testaccio

Andreotti

This is the most popular cake shop in Testaccio. It has a large selection of cornetti (croissants), cakes, and even savory nibbles, and the Sachertorte is considered one of the best in Rome. Delicious desserts include monte bianco (made with chestnut purée, whipped cream, and sometimes meringue), and mimosa, a fluffy yellow cake named after the yellow flower.

VIA OSTIENSE 51B, 06 575 0773

Mercato di Testaccio

Romans who live near Testaccio do all of their food shopping at this market and plenty of people from other parts of the city make the trip here because of the quality and variety of the produce on sale. Tourists are few and far between here as Romans get on with the serious business of food shopping. The meat and fish are wonderfully fresh, there's a huge selection of fruit and vegetables, and bread stands groan under the weight of their bread rolls, focaccia, ciabatta, pastries, long, French-style loaves, and fruit tarts. Like all the main markets in the city, it is open in the mornings from Monday through to Saturday and most of the traders start packing up around 1.30pm.

PIAZZA TESTACCIO

Canestro

Canestro was one of the first shops in Rome to specialize in organic food. You can pick up specialty bread made with a variety of flours, and bags of vacuum-packed whole grains and flours. This is one of the few places in the city to sell grano saraceno (buckwheat). The Italian name throws light upon the origins of the different flours that were introduced into Italy by marauding pirates in the Mediterranean. Arabs brought grano saraceno and granturco (cornflour) came with the Turks. You can stock up on Canestro's organic cheeses, meats, and various forms of soy (soya), as well as other health foods and even herbal beauty products.

Via Luca della Robbia 12,
06 574 6287

Carla Specialità Gastronomiche

The care taken over the choice of produce is the only criterion in this traditional and unpretentious store. A small selection of vegetables has recently been added to their range of stock, making life much easier for those who want to do their shopping after work, by which time Testaccio's central market has already closed.

Piazza Testaccio 24, 06 574 2569

Shops in Testaccio

Pescheria Ostiense

This large fish store opens at 6am every morning. The prices are very reasonable and the farmed fish are clearly marked so that you know what you are buying. There are always mussels and clams, and the squid and cuttlefish are great value.
VIA DEL PORTO FLUVIALE 67C, 06 674 1108

La Fromagerie

Enoteca Palombi next door owns this relatively new store which has a fantastic choice of regional Italian and imported cheeses. The salumeria is equally good and there is a good selection of more luxurious foods including bottarga (pressed dried tuna or mullet roe), truffles in season, Spanish hams, and a large selection of teas stored in smart green metal containers.
PIAZZA TESTACCIO 35, 06 5725 0185

Il Mioi Fornaio di Romeo Cantarelli

Romans come here to this bakery for the small rolls covered with poppy or sesame seeds, the great wheels of Calabrian pane casareccio (round, dark bread baked in a wood oven), and loaves made with unusual grains. Their pizza a taglio is delicious and they have a wonderful selection of cakes and cookies. You can even order bread to be baked in a certain way to avoid food allergies.
PIAZZA BERNINI 2, 06 578 0746

Palombi

Originally a wine shop, Palombi is now the largest enoteca in Testaccio. You'll find wine and beers from all over the world, as well as foods not available at La Fromagerie next door, such as rice, pulses, preserves, and chocolate, as well as imported products like sour cream.
PIAZZA TESTACCIO 38, 06 574 6122

Passi

Passi is another wonderful Testaccio bakery, selling cakes, bread, and trays of crusty pizza, either plain (bianca), with tomato (rossa), or topped with sliced potatoes and rosemary. The home-made cakes include tarts (crostate) with sour cherries, or apricots, ricotta tart, and what is called "plum cake" in Italy, but which is really sponge cake with no plums in sight!
VIA MASTRO GIORGIO 87, 06 574 6563

Ne Arte Ne Parte

Before the Roman actor Ricky Memphis took over this trattoria, it had had a rather checkered past. Now its fortunes have taken an upward turn. The dishes are the typical Roman favorites like pasta cacio e pepe, abbacchio scottadito (grilled or barbecued lamb chops), and some robust *quinto quarto* (variety meats or offal) recipes like coda alla vaccinara (oxtail stew). Evenings here are lively and noisy with a party atmosphere, and it is advisable to make a reservation, whereas at lunchtime the trattoria has a more sedate clientele of shop assistants, office workers, and people who have just finished food shopping in the nearby Testaccio food market.

Via Luca della Robbia 15, 06 575 0279

Torricella

The good value offered by this large trattoria is remarkable. The menu is extensive but the simplest dishes are the best. Augusto and his sister, Michelina, come from Abruzzo, a region known for its good food. They serve some of their native potato dishes as well as an excellent cacio e pepe, gricia (pasta with bacon and garlic), and tonnarelli with shrimp, zucchini (courgettes), and small red tomatoes from Pachino, in Sicily.

Via Evangelista Torricelli 2, 06 574 6311

Vesuvio

The chef here leaves the dough to rise for eight hours, which makes the resulting pizza base deliciously crispy. He uses quality ingredients for the toppings, so the best of Naples and Rome is to be found in this pizzeria.

Via Chiabrera 71, 06 540 5634

Checchino dal 1887

The restaurant Checchino started life as a wine shop in one of the storage caves cut into the side of Monte Testaccio. In 1887 the owner, Checchino, obtained a license to serve simple food with the wine, and when the new slaughterhouse was opened nearby in 1890 the restaurant's success was assured. The slaughterhouse workers gave the variety meats and offcuts (offal) that were part of their pay to Ferminia, Checchino's daughter, to cook. She invented many ingenious dishes, including the famous coda alla vaccinara (oxtail stew) and pajata (intestines cooked in tomato sauce).

Today Checcino has become a fashionable restaurant, run by descendants of the same family. Although the *quinto quarto* dishes can still be found on the menu, they are lighter, and there are many other excellent suggestions for those who do not share the robust tastes of the past, such as involtini di carciofi (veal rolls filled with artichokes).

Via di Monte Testaccio 30, 06 574 3816

Saltimbocca alla Romana

Veal with ham and sage

In this recipe, the hidden sage leaves are said to make the meat "jump in the mouth" (*saltimbocca*). It is a very popular dish, quick to prepare at home, and is found on the menu of many Roman trattorias. I often serve this with puréed potatoes.

SERVES 4
PREPARATION TIME: 10 MINUTES
COOKING TIME: 5–7 MINUTES

8 veal escalopes, total weight about 500g/1lb 2oz
salt and freshly ground black pepper
8 sage leaves
4 thin slices of prosciutto, halved crosswise
50g/2oz/¼ cup butter
4tbsp dry white wine

Season the veal escalopes with salt and pepper and place a sage leaf then half a slice of prosciutto on top of each one, securing them in place with a wooden toothpick.

Melt the butter in a large skillet, add the veal, and fry gently over a medium heat until the meat is brown. Turn the pieces over and cook briefly with the prosciutto side in contact with the hot butter. After a few minutes, pour the wine into the skillet and tilt the pan so that it mixes with the cooking juices.

Carefully remove the veal and arrange on a warm serving plate. Return the skillet to the stove, increase the heat to high and stir 1 tablespoon of hot water into the wine sauce. Try to scrape up the bits stuck to the pan — they will add extra flavor. Cook for 2–3 minutes until the sauce has reduced a little, then spoon the sauce over the veal slices.

Quadrucci e Piselli

Pasta and peas

In spring, when the small tender peas first appear, they are so good people want to eat them as often as possible, in as many guises as possible, as long as their delicate flavor is not masked. In Testaccio market, the older market traders sit shucking the peas with still-nimble fingers, while their children get on with the job of selling them. If you are in a hurry you can buy small bags of ready-shelled peas, but usually it is a greater pleasure to buy them in the pod so that you can munch the odd pea as you sit at home shelling them.

SERVES 4
PREPARATION TIME: 20 MINUTES
COOKING TIME: 25 MINUTES

2tbsp olive oil
1 onion, diced
1 garlic clove, peeled and finely sliced
½ celery stick, finely chopped
2 slices bacon, finely chopped
300g/10½oz/2 cups shelled peas
1tbsp flat-leaf parsley, chopped
salt and freshly ground black pepper
1½ liters/2½ pints/6¼ cups light chicken, veal or vegetable stock
300g/10oz quadrucci (1cm/ ½ inch squares of fresh or dried egg pasta)
6tbsp freshly grated Parmesan cheese

Heat the oil in a large saucepan and gently cook the onion, garlic, celery, and bacon until soft. Add the peas, parsley, and seasoning and cook them gently for 10 minutes.

In a separate pan bring the stock to the boil. Once boiling, pour the stock into the pan with the vegetables. Bring this to the boil, and, when boiling, add the pasta to the pan. Cook the pasta according to the instructions on the pack until al dente.

Serve at once on warm plates with a generous sprinkling of Parmesan over each serving.

Monte Testaccio

It used to be possible to climb over the hill known as Monte Testaccio picking up shards of pottery, and in *A Traveller in Rome*, H.V. Morton describes how he filled his pockets with pieces of broken amphorae, imagining that perhaps these jars had contained olives eaten by Augustus or nibbled by Horace. Today it's no longer possible to walk over the hill and, although rather late in the day, this priceless site is being given proper recognition.

Rome is built on seven natural hills: Palatine, Capitoline, Quirinal, Viminal, Esquiline, Caelian, and Aventine. There is also an eighth hill, but this one was artificially created. Monte Testaccio, near the Piramide in Testaccio, is a triangular hill which is roughly one kilometer around the base and about forty-five meters high. Instead of being formed of earth, it is made up of about eighty-six million broken amphorae.

The origins of the hill date back to the first century, in the early days of the Roman Empire, and the story of how the hill was gradually formed over the following three hundred years from the waste products of trade is intriguing. During the time of the Roman Empire, the cheapest and easiest way to bring merchandise from the many parts of the vast Empire to Rome was by sea. Great triremes (galleys with three banks of oars) brought cargoes of oil and grain from Spain and North Africa, using first the port of Pozzuoli, near Naples, and later Ostia, Rome's port. From Ostia the goods were then transferred to smaller boats or rafts which were towed by oxen or teams of slaves up the River Tiber to Rome. Great warehouses were established along the river at the foot of the Aventine hill to store these goods.

The large amphorae used for the sea voyage were seventy to eighty centimeters high, with a diameter of sixty centimeters, and could hold up to seventy kilos of oil. When the shipments arrived in Rome, the oil was decanted into smaller containers for easy distribution and the terracotta amphorae were then broken up and stacked systematically in an open space nearby. The lower part of the amphora was used as a base to give stability to the potsherd dump, and the necks and handles were laid on the top. Each fresh load was then covered with a little earth to avoid unpleasant odors. Over the centuries this hill became covered with light vegetation and people began to forget the origins of the hill. Centuries later caves were cut into the hill to store the wine brought in by horse and cart from the wine region, Castelli Romani, because the insulating properties of the terracotta and the space between the broken pieces kept the temperature between seven and ten degrees centigrade. As a result of this readily available chilled storage area, a few simple wine shops began to open in the area.

In the last few years, teams from the universities of Barcelona and Rome have excavated a small area of Monte Testaccio, and from the inscriptions baked into the amphorae and the shipping details painted on them (the dry atmosphere had kept the ink completely legible), their origins were discernible. It was discovered that eighty percent of the amphorae had traveled from Andalusia, Spain's great olive oil producing region, fifteen percent from North Africa, and five percent from Gaul and southern Italy. These amphorae had probably been used for the transportation of wine.

Monte Testaccio is now protected as a national treasure and gone are the days when carnival games involved men and animals scrambling down the hill with a complete disregard for the treasures below them. In modern Rome young people crowd to the nightclubs that have grown up in Testaccio, and as they dance the night away they are oblivious to the centuries-old history of this *quartiere*.

Landmarks

This area is dominated by the tall, white Piramide (below), which is the burial site of a Roman praetor (a form of magistrate in ancient Rome) named Caius Cestius, who lived in the first century BC. Cestius had delusions of grandeur and, after a visit to Egypt, decided to emulate the style of the pharaohs when building his tomb. The tomb became dwarfed by the surrounding trees and debris, but was cleaned and the base excavated when a wall was built around the nearby Protestant Cemetery.

Cimitero Protestante

The Protestant Cemetery first appeared in the late eighteenth century as a place of burial for English visitors, because the Popes had barred non-Catholics from being buried in Catholic graveyards. The ashes of the English poet Percy Bysshe Shelley were buried here after he drowned in 1822, at the age of only twenty-nine. Another English poet, John Keats, has his tomb here (above). He came to Rome in 1821 in a last attempt to save his life, as he knew that he was seriously ill with consumption. He died in Rome a few months later at the age of twenty-five. By his side lies Joseph Severn, the friend who nursed him devotedly through his illness, and who many years later returned to Rome as British Consul. The grave is surrounded by trees and the scent of violets, making it seem more like an English country churchyard, especially when the birdsong seems to block out the roar of nearby traffic.

The cemetery, which is administered by a committee of foreign diplomats, is now the burial place of Protestants of many other nationalities too and contains about two and a half thousand graves. Further down the road is the British War Cemetery for soldiers who died in and around Rome in World War II.

Garbatella

Within easy reach of Testaccio proper is Garbatella. The serried ranks of the unadorned apartment blocks here were not an appealing sight but the original idea was delightful. Small houses were built in a cluster with little balconies and courtyards for the local workers. Today, after some modernization, these amber-colored buildings are very desirable. Before these houses were built, Garbatella had been an undeveloped zone where shepherds used to bring their sheep to graze in winter, using a central building to make and sell Pecorino cheese.

Mattatoio

When the Mattatoio opened in 1890 it was the most modern slaughterhouse in Europe. It was a grandiose scheme, complete with a railway line and other innovations, so architects were invited to bid for the right to design the final project. The great entrance gates were embellished with sculpture, and cast-iron and travertine were used throughout the complex, which covered more than one hundred thousand square meters. Nearly half of the space consisted of covered areas and the slaughterhouse provided work for hundreds of local people.

The Mattatoio closed in 1975 and the building is now subject to a conservation order. Different plans are being considered for its redevelopment but to date no final decision has been made. It has housed some special exhibitions and the whole area comes alive at night, when young people flock to the bars and nightclubs which have sprung up here. Legacies of the slaughterhouse include the quintessential Roman *quinto quarto* recipes, which came about when the workers received part of their wages as offcuts of meat. A further legacy is that the Mattatoio is a fine example of how art can be used to adorn and improve even the most humble places of work.

Mura Aurelle

The Roman Emperor Aurelian built a massive wall about twelve miles long in order to keep out invading barbarian hordes. Today much of the wall is still intact, because the attackers used the more effective strategy of sabotaging Rome's water supply by damaging the aqueducts. Parts of the wall can still be seen near piazza di Porta San Paolo.

San Paolo fuori le Mura

Further south from the main area of Testaccio is this beautiful church whose name means "St. Paul outside the Walls". Until St. Peter's was built, this was the largest church in Christendom. A fire in 1823 nearly destroyed the basilica but it was quickly rebuilt and many original features survived, including the bronze Holy door (right), which dates from the eleventh century.

Pages 158–9: the Byzantine-style mosaics on the apse in the Church of San Paolo fuori le Mura were made around 1120 by specialist craftsmen from Venice.

Vaticano & Prati

Although this area is dominated by the dome of St. Peter's, and the attractions of the Vatican Museums and the Sistine Chapel, food is what draws many Romans to Prati. Two of the city's best food stores, Castroni and Franchi, on the main shopping street via Cola di Rienzo, are where Romans from all over the city stock up on prosciutto, cheese, salami, and olive oil. Further up the River Tiber the ancient Ponte Milvio marks the start of the street market selling fresh produce where Romans from the north of the city come to shop.

Vaticano & Prati

In these districts you can see a great range of historical ages and architectural styles as you move away from the Roman Empire in the historic center and move up the River Tiber to find the bald announcement "Mussolini Dux" on the obelisk Mussolini commissioned outside the soccer stadium, the Stadio Olimpico. You pass from Renaissance and Baroque magnificence to the simplicity of the ancient and humble bridge, Ponte Milvio.

It is strange but I always feel closer to classical Rome than to ecclesiastical Rome. I studied Latin at school until I was eighteen years old, and perhaps it is the pages of Livy and Virgil that make me feel at home in ancient Rome. The Vatican and St. Peter's fill me with awe but they put me at a distance. The only time I have ever felt at ease was when I was privileged enough to receive permission to do some special research in the Vatican Library. I suppose a theologian would reply that one should not feel at ease with God.

The narrow little roads around St. Peter's, the Borgo area, have a different feel and you

can sense the hum of everyday life. Ordinary people live here and go about their daily business like their fellow Romans, who breathe less hallowed air, away from the magnificence of the Vatican.

Before Italy was unified the neighborhood called Prati was once just open fields and meadows (*prati*), but careful planning and construction led to the ordered grid of streets that you see today. In ancient Rome all the oblations of wine, poured to the Lares and Penates at mealtimes by centuries of pagan Romans, ensured a benign presence in the following ages. Prati might not have a benign presence from the past but the modern god of shopping rules here and ensures happy purchases. Prati is a great shopping area for shoes, handbags, and clothes in all price ranges and there are many tempting *profumerie* selling cosmetics and perfumes. A Saturday morning spent window-shopping in via Cola di Rienzo, a slightly extravagant purchase, and then you are ready for more self-indulgence and pleasure in the fabulous food stores.

The *gastronomia* Franchi is right next to the Aladdin's cave that is Castroni. Both of theses food stores are irresistible and fortunately, or unfortunately, they both take credit cards! Franchi has a great *salumeria* counter piled high with every form of temptation, with cheeses from all over Italy, France, and Great Britain, and many different hams and salames. Deeper into the store are prepared dishes like stuffed tomatoes and splendid-looking shelled prawns, and Rome's favorite fried nibbles, which are prepared in batches. There is a wonderful selection of wines and many people come here for a gastronomic snack. Castroni sells groceries

from all over the world and has the cure for any form of global homesickness. Where else in Rome could you find Cadbury chocolate and Marmite, or Aunt Jemima's pancake mix and peanut butter? There are all the ingredients needed for Mexican or Japanese cooking and every imaginable spice and dried herb. As Romans become more and more interested in ethnic food they come here not only for the top quality Italian ingredients like olive oil and balsamic vinegar, but also for some more exotic food items. Across the road from Castroni there is a covered food market selling fish, meat, fruit, and vegetables and not too far away, in via Germanico, there is the restaurant Girarrosto which serves the best beef in Rome — the steak alone justifies a visit to this neighborhood.

Further up the River Tiber from here the sports complex and soccer stadium, the Stadio Olimpico, has its own living gods. Here in modern Italy soccer is a religion and passions run high, with the greatest heat reserved for the rivalry between the city's two teams Roma and Lazio. To the uninitiated this passion seems inexplicable but it is an important aspect of daily life for many Romans.

Further north from the stadium is the ancient bridge across the Tiber, Ponte Milvio, where I feel more on home ground. Food is the great common denominator here and I wander around the street market here happily buying my vegetables and fresh herbs. If you come here, make sure you take the opportunity to walk halfway across Ponte Milvio, then look back down the river to take in the view of ancient Rome and St. Peter's, and think of all the events the city has witnessed.

Shops in Vaticano & Prati

Apistica Romana

This is probably the only shop in Rome that specializes in honey and bee products; there must be over twenty different flavors of honey. They also sell honeycomb, pappa reale (royal jelly), and other beauty preparations made from bee products.

Via Ulpiano 50/57, 06 686 8004

La Bottega del Carne

This temple to great quality meat sells goose and duck as well as the more common beef, lamb, and pork, which all come from small livestock farms. You can order game in season. The same pride that is shown in the fresh meat is evident in the array of pre-prepared meat dishes.

Via Avezzana 17, 06 321 791

Castroni

This is the main store in the Castroni empire, selling one of the best selections of olive oils and vinegars in Rome, plus other reputable Italian grocery items. The specialty, though, is imported ethnic products in jars, packets, and cans, with a vast range of spices, herbs, flours, and grains, while at the bar you can sample their selection of tea and coffee.

Via Cola di Rienzo 196, 06 6874 3382

La Compagnia del Pane

It's a joy to come here because it's obvious that the whole family works with enthusiasm and passion. In fact, this is the second bakery that the family runs, and it hasn't been open for very long, whereas the original store dates back to 1929. The shelves contain traditional breads from Lariano, Genzano, and Terni, as well as less traditional (but no less delicious) breads made with olives or walnuts. They also sell other baked goods such as cornetti (croissants) and pizza bianca.

Via Fabio Massimo 87/89, 06 324 1605

La Confetteria

As well as chocolates, this divine candy and chocolate store also sells sugared almonds, and enticing jars of preserves. This is *the* place in Rome to buy fabulous marrons glacés.

Via Lucrezia Caro 24/28,

Fattoria dell'Alento

If you love cheese then this is the store for you. The main products are cheeses produced at the family's farm in the Salento area, including mozzarella di Bufala made from the milk from their own buffalo herd. This is one of the few stores where you can still find cheeses in traditional shapes like plaits and knots. Ricotta, scamorze (soft, distinctively shaped cow's milk cheese), and caciocavallo (a cheese made in a similar way to mozzarella, but semi-hard and matured for longer) are all available.

Via Orazio 17, 06 322 7287

Il Gianfornaio

This legendary store is always packed. Every sort of bread imaginable is sold here, and the pizza a metro (pizza served by the meter) is eagerly snapped up as it slides through the baker's hatch to the front of the store. Baskets of bread can be ordered for special occasions; my Roman friends order baskets filled with small rolls colored with green, pink, and yellow vegetable dyes.

Piazzale Ponte Milvio 35, 06 333 3472

Mercato Piazza dell'Unità

This covered market has one entrance at the back and one on via Cola di Rienzo. It is on the other side of the road (going towards piazza Risorgimento) from the wonderful Franchi and Castroni specialty food stores, so you can combine a visit to them for your grocery shopping with a trip to the market for the freshest vegetables, fruit, and fish.

Piazza dell'Unità

Mercato Ponte Milvio

This street market is quite a way further north up the River Tiber from Prati. Running parallel to the river, the market is great for vegetables and fruit, although be prepared for the fact that it is fairly expensive. The stands nearer the lovely pedestrian footbridge tend to have the best quality produce.

Ponte Milvio

Mondi

Mondi is a Roman institution where everything is a feast for the eyes. The cakes are legendary and the ice cream practically has its own fan club. There are also delicious miniature savory rolls and buns, and small versions of traditional desserts like monte bianco (with chestnut, whipped cream, and meringue), profiteroles, and Sicilian cassata, all crying out to be bought.

Via Flaminia Vecchia 468, 06 333 6466

Franchi

Customers from all over Rome flock here to what could be described as Rome's top food store. Locals stock up on prosciutto, salami, and regional Italian and French cheeses. There is a whole range of specialty rice and pasta, as well as luxury foods like truffles and caviar. At one end of the store a superior tavola calda sells fried treats like fillets of baccalà, zucchini (courgette) flowers, and artichokes, and delicious prepared dishes that you can take home include salmon mousse, vegetable fritters, ravioli, and lasagne.

Via Cola di Rienzo 200, 06 687 4651

Stracetti alla Rughetta

Slivers of beef or veal with arugula (rocket)

Stracetti means "little rags", and this easy modern recipe uses thin slices of beef, similar to those served raw as carpaccio. The tangy arugula (rocket) makes it a firm favorite, and it is found on most trattoria menus; it is particularly popular with Roman women, because they believe it is not too high in calories. If the meat is pre-sliced, the recipe takes all of five minutes to prepare. If possible, have the butcher slice the meat for you; if you have to do it yourself, put the unsliced meat in the freezer for 30–40 minutes first, which will make it easier to slice.

SERVES 4

PREPARATION TIME: 10 MINUTES

COOKING TIME: 4 MINUTES

2tbsp olive oil

500g/1lb 2oz fillet of beef
  or veal, cut into wafer
  thin slices

salt and freshly ground
  black pepper

1 large bunch of wild arugula
  (rocket)

Heat the olive oil in a large skillet set over a low heat. Add the slices of beef or veal and cook, stirring, for 2 minutes.

Season with salt and pepper and add the arugula leaves. Cover the skillet and cook the meat with the arugula over a low heat for another 2 minutes.

Remove from the skillet and serve immediately. A few extra drops of olive oil can be added before serving, if desired.

Pasticcio di Maccheroni con Melanzane

Baked pasta with eggplant (aubergine)

In Rome eggplants (aubergines) used to be called *marignani*. In the nineteenth century, Vatican clergymen who were sent out of the city on special missions were dressed in voluminous eggplant-colored cloaks. Mischievous Romans nicknamed these clergymen *marignani*.

SERVES 6

PREPARATION TIME: 50 MINUTES

COOKING TIME: 25 MINUTES

4 eggplants (aubergine), sliced

coarse salt

olive oil for frying

400g/14oz ziti or rigatoni

6 fresh basil leaves, torn into
  small pieces

300g/10oz mozzarella, sliced
  thinly

50g/2oz/½ cup freshly grated
  Parmesan

2tbsp breadcrumbs made from
  day-old bread

900ml/32fl oz/4 cups fresh
  tomato sauce (see Penne
  Arrabbiata recipe)

Layer the slices of eggplant with coarse salt in a colander and leave for 30 minutes. Meanwhile, make the tomato sauce according to the recipe on page 109.

Once the 30 minutes are up, rinse the eggplant slices well and dry with paper towels. Set a large skillet over a medium heat, add oil, and fry the eggplant in batches until golden and just tender. Drain on paper towels.

Preheat the oven to 200°C/400°F/gas mark 6. Bring a large pan of lightly salted water to the boil, add the pasta, and cook according to the instructions on the pack until it is pliable but not fully cooked. Drain and immediately toss with the tomato sauce and torn basil leaves.

Oil a deep ovenproof dish and put in a thin layer of pasta in tomato sauce. Cover with a layer of eggplant and a few slices of mozzarella. Sprinkle on some Parmesan and add another layer of pasta. Continue, making at least three layers, finishing with a layer of eggplant then mozzarella. Combine the remaining Parmesan with the breadcrumbs and sprinkle the mixture on top. Bake in the oven for 25 minutes, or until golden and bubbling. Remove the dish from the oven and then leave it to stand for 5–10 minutes before serving.

Angeli al Borgo

This modest pizzeria between Castel Sant'Angelo and San Pietro serves crisp pizza and freshly fried supplì (savory rice balls), crocchette, zucchini (courgette) flowers, and baccalà fillets. There is a selection of vegetable antipasto but no main courses.

BORGO ANGELICO 28, 06 686 9674

Antica Dogana

In warm weather this is a perfect place for lunch as the garden fronts the river bank, and you can sit back with a glass of wine and contemplate the menu, glancing up from time to time as a canoeist skulls past. Meat dishes are cooked on the large open grill and maiolino (roast suckling pig) can be ordered in advance.

VIA CAPOPRATI 10, 06 3751 8558

L'Arcangelo

In this comfortable Prati restaurant you can enjoy an excellent Roman tasting menu with all the traditional favorites cooked with masterly skill, or you could go for more creative dishes such as a molded octopus salad with citrus fruit, or the foie gras menu.

VIA G. BELLI 59, 06 321 0992

Cacio e Pepe da Gianni

Tables spill out of this small trattoria on to the street. The specialty, as the name suggests, is tonnarelli cacio e pepe. The portions are generous, but leave room for the tasty version of polpettone (meat loaf), or melanzane alla parmigiana.

VIA AVEZZANA 11, 06 321 7268

Dante Taberna de' Gracchi

They have been serving consistently good food in this family-run restaurant for many years. There isn't time to tire of the menu as new dishes are always being added. Traditional mezze maniche pasta (large tubes of pasta) and the manzo stracotto con sedano (slow-cooked beef with celery), remain popular. Traditional Roman beef dishes need long, slow cooking but as fewer and fewer restaurants have the time to slow-cook, finding a restaurant which still does is a bonus.

VIA DEI GRACCHI 266, 06 321 3126

Il Matriciano

This historic trattoria has been serving traditional Roman dishes for the past hundred years. Most of the customers are regulars and there is a happy, relaxed atmosphere as they tuck into their favorite pasta dish, the classic Matriciana, of course.

VIA DEI GRACCHI 55, 06 321 2327

Da Benito e Gilberto

Reservations are essential for dinner in this small, noisy trattoria where excellent fish is served at reasonable prices. Benito's son, Gilberto, is now the sole proprietor, and the service and cooking are still as reliable as ever. There is a tantalizing display of fish at the entrance and you can choose your fish and discuss whether it should be baked in a salt crust, cooked in acqua pazza (water flavored with chiles and tomato), or just broiled. Other seafood choices are sautéed mussels or raw shellfish for a first course, then perhaps fritto di gamberi e calamari (fried shrimp and squid), or a pasta dish like tagliolini alla pescatora (tagliolini with fisherman's sauce). A simple wine list and home-made desserts complete the meal.

VIA DEL FALCO 19, 06 686 7709

L'Ortica

This is my favorite Neapolitan restaurant in Rome. It has an unusual setting on the top of a one-story supermarket, but in the stifling summer heat the huge roof terrace is a green oasis of calm. There is a quiet, unstudied elegance that is difficult to find in Naples itself. The superb mozzarella that is brought up from Campania each day can be followed by a delicate gattò di patate (potato cake) or pasta with pesto. For dessert try authentic babà (a cake similar to a rum baba or savarin), or pastiera (a tart made with wheat grains, ricotta, and candied fruits).

Via Flaminia Vecchia 573, 06 333 8709

Velando

Patrizia Podetti has brought her recipes with her down from the north of Italy to the heart of the Vatican area of the city to tease and intrigue with their novelty. As an example, this is probably the only place in Rome to serve pizzocheri (buckwheat ribbon pasta). Duck with chestnuts and prunes might not be traditionally Roman, but is a dish well worth ordering.

Borgo Vittorio 26, 06 6880 9955

Pages 170–1: the impressive dome of St. Peter's is visible from all over the city. It is even more beautiful when seen from below.

Giarrosto Toscano

This restaurant opened its doors in 1938 and is now run by the third generation of the Bruni family. Some restaurant critics think menus should change but I come here to eat what I always eat here. At the entrance there is a tall glass display case storing and presenting good Tuscan meat, and a large grill stands nearby. For antipasto, there is a plate of mixed salami, including finnochiona (with fennel seeds), and mozzarella. Next, there are fine pasta dishes or perhaps farro soup, which is made with an old variety of grain that is becoming popular again. As they serve the best beef in Rome here, for main course the obvious choice is a grilled fiorentino steak (on the bone) with some white beans. Home-made desserts include a delicious torta di ricotta.

Via Germanico 56, 06 3972 5717

Peperoni alla Romana

Bell peppers with tomatoes

This can be made with red or green bell peppers, or a mixture of the two. The red bell peppers are sweet, while the green bell peppers have a rather bitter flavor. Romans tend to like bitter vegetables.

SERVES 4
PREPARATION TIME: 10 MINUTES
COOKING TIME: 20 MINUTES

6 bell peppers	3 tomatoes, peeled and seeded
4tbsp olive oil	salt and freshly ground
1 onion, finely sliced	black pepper

Place the peppers under a hot broiler (grill) or on a hot barbecue so that the skins blister and burn.

Put to cool in a closed paper or plastic bag, then peel off the skins and discard the seeds and membranes. Cut the peppers into strips about 3cm/1¼ inches wide.

Heat the oil in a skillet and then add the onion. Gently cook the onion until soft. Add the tomatoes, season, and simmer for 10 minutes. Stir in the bell peppers, cook gently for a few minutes, then remove from the heat.

Serve at room temperature.

Tagliatelle alla Papalina

Pope's pasta

This recipe was made in La Cisterna trattoria for Cardinal Pacelli because it was his favorite pasta dish. When he became Pope Pius XII in 1939 the restaurateurs dedicated it to him.

SERVES 4
PREPARATION TIME: 15 MINUTES
COOKING TIME: 15 MINUTES

100g/3½ oz/½ cup butter	100g/3½ oz/1 cup freshly grated
1 small onion, chopped	Parmesan
200g/7oz prosciutto, cut	salt and freshly ground
into ribbons	black pepper
500g/1lb 2oz tagliatelle	small handful fresh basil
4 eggs	leaves to garnish
200ml/7fl oz/⅞ cup light	Parmesan shavings to garnish
(single) cream	

Put a large saucepan of water on to boil for the pasta.

Meanwhile, melt half the butter and gently cook the onion until it becomes transparent. Add the prosciutto and allow to warm through.

When the water comes to the boil add a little salt and cook the pasta according to the pack instructions until it is al dente.

While the pasta is cooking beat the eggs and cream with half the grated Parmesan. Melt the remaining butter in a large pan and stir in the egg mixture. Remove from heat immediately. Season to taste.

Drain the pasta and stir into the egg mixture. Now stir in the ham and onions and keep stirring until the eggs coagulate to form a thick yellow cream. Add black pepper, some basil leaves, and Parmesan shavings and serve at once. Put the remaining grated Parmesan in a bowl for those who want to add more to their pasta.

Landmarks

This area of Rome is dominated by the dome of St. Peter's, which acts as a homing beacon when exploring the city. If you have a faulty sense of direction its reassuring presence will help you get your bearings. The other main landmark apart from St. Peter's and the Vatican Museums is Castel Sant'Angelo. From here you can follow the River Tiber past a Gothic church and all the way up to the historic Ponte Milvio.

Basilica di San Pietro

The great cupola of St. Peter's was designed by Michelangelo although he did not live to see the work completed in 1593. The massive Vatican walls, with a circumference of three kilometers, were started by Pope Leo IV in AD 846, a year after the Saracens had successfully attacked and plundered Rome. The walls have been reinforced and repaired over the centuries. The present Porta Santo Spirito, the last door on the right of the facade, was built in the sixteenth century and is ceremoniously opened in an Annus Jubileus, or Holy Year; the last time this happened was Christmas Eve 1999, with Pope John Paul II performing the ceremony.

The Vatican Museums, which used to be papal palaces, have their entrance in viale Vaticano. An impressive 1930s staircase (left) spirals up to the museums which are full of art treasures, with Egyptian, Greek, Etruscan, and Roman antiquities. Many people in the long queues outside are waiting in line with the sole intention of seeing Michelangelo's Sistine Chapel. A small passageway, il Passetto, links the Vatican to Castel Sant'Angelo as an escape route for the Pope in times of danger.

Pages 178–9: you can glimpse the Vatican Gardens from the windows of the museum. They follow the formal Italian style of rectangular parterres and box hedges.

Castel Sant'Angelo

Castel Sant'Angelo (below) started life in AD 139 as Hadrian's mausoleum. Around one hundred and forty years later the walls were built up and incorporated into the defensive ring the Emperor Aurelian built about the city. In its time Castel Sant'Angelo has been a palace, a stronghold, and a prison, and there are gruesome stories of prisoners disappearing down oubliettes, to be disposed of in the River Tiber. The castle gets its name from the bronze statue of St. Michael on the top.

Piazza Cavour

Piazza Cavour was named after the great Piemontese statesman Camillo Cavour, who orchestrated the unification of Italy, along with Garibaldi and Mazzini. A statue of Cavour was erected in 1895. A contemporary wit asked if Cavour and Mazzini had quarreled because his statue has its back to Mazzini's statue in piazza Mazzini opposite.

Ponte Milvio

Ponte Milvio is one of the oldest bridges over the River Tiber — the original wooden bridge was built three or four hundred years BC and was the site of Constantine's conversion to Christianity. One of Rome's good outdoor food markets starts at the bridge.

Prati

Until Italy was unified the area known as Prati was simply meadows. The swampy land was frequently flooded and there was no urban development until about 1880 when some military barracks were built. The center of Rome further south could not contain the great influx of people flocking to the new capital and so it was decided to turn the meadows into a new Roman district or *rione*, and many of the streets were named after great Ancient Roman writers.

Via Cola di Rienzo

Running all the way from the Vatican to piazza del Popolo, this great fashionable shopping street used to be home to elegant Caffè Latour until it unfortunately closed in the 1970s. Today it is still a great place to go shopping, with well-known food stores Castroni and Franchi as well as numerous stores selling clothes, shoes, handbags, jewelry, and other accessories.

Fuori Roma

Romans traditionally flee the heat of the summer and head to the historic towns of the Castelli Romani, south of Rome. Here they dine on dishes with traditional Castelli ingredients like *porchetta* (roast suckling pig), small wild strawberries, and funghi porcini (ceps), and drink crisp wines from Frascati in restaurants with open-air terraces. The area is known for its small, independent food shops which sell high quality bread and meat, and there are several independent cheese-producers who make cheese to send up to the city every day.

Fuori Roma

The small wine producing hilltowns to the south of Rome are known as the Colline Albine or the Castelli Romani. The Roman emperors made these hills their summer retreat to escape from the stifling heat of the city, and built many villas and temples in this area. In the seventeenth century aristocratic families followed suit, building elegant villas complete with beautiful gardens and parks. In 1626 Pope Urban VIII rebuilt the old Savelli Castle in Castel Gandolfo, which the Church then owned, and it has since been the Pope's official summer palace and residence.

Ordinary Romans have also always sought to escape the city's humid summer heat, and the practice of taking a day or evening trip to the Castelli is well established. As well as the cooling breezes and fresh air, good food and wine are the lure. Going *fuori porta*, outside the city gate, has always involved eating and drinking. The first Rome–Frascati steam train made it possible to do the trip in a day. People often made themselves a packed lunch to be eaten at rustic tables set under trees, where they could buy local wine from the barrel. The last train back to Rome was known as the *tropéa*, or drunken train. With the first

trattorias came the tradition of the *abbuffata*, from the Roman dialect word *buffare*, which means "to blow" or "to puff", and which refers to gorging oneself on food.

Today many of the Castelli towns have their own particular food specialties. In Genzano it is bread, in Nemi *fragoline del bosco* (cultivated small wild strawberries), and around all the woods, especially at Nemi and Rocca di Papa, various wild mushrooms are sold by the roadside, as well as by safer, more orthodox vendors. Every year there are reports of people being poisoned by eating funghi they hadn't recognized as dangerous, so you do need to know what you are doing.

You can find a festival celebrating food somewhere in the Castelli every month of the year, although these festivals have become more oriented towards tourism in recent years. In May, Velletri has an artichoke festival and on 23 June, Frascati holds a festival of lumache (snails). At this festival you should also keep an eye open for the pupazze, the honey pastries in the form of a woman with three breasts, which are a legacy of pagan fertility rites. On the third Sunday in July, Castel Gandolfo celebrates peaches at the sagra delle pesche and on the first Sunday of September, Arricia celebrates suckling pig at the sagra della porchetta. The third Sunday in September in Genzano is the time for the sagra del pane casareccio, a celebration of bread, and on the last Sunday in October in Rocca di Papa, there is an autumnal celebration of the humble castagna (chestnut).

The Castelli Romani have always supplied the city with table wine and the Ancient Roman writers were eloquent in their praise of its quality. The wine used to be transported in barrels by horse and cart and even thirty

years ago most trattorias in the city had a cold store dispenser with two taps, one for white wine and one for red wine. For many Romans visiting the Castelli for Sunday lunch, quantity was more important than quality and the kindest thing to be said about the Frascati and Marino loose wines was that they did not travel well so they needed to be drunk *in situ*. Today there is a varying degree of quality among these wines and it is worth trying several different bottles to find one that you particularly like.

Traditionally Romans have always drunk white wines and the wines with the "DOC" label are all white. This causes a certain amount of puzzlement among international wine experts since the rich volcanic soil of the Colli Albani is ideal for red wine, and they feel that this should be a predominantly red wine area. Gradually some of the white vines are being replaced with red, and today there are several serious wine growers working in this area producing some outstanding wines.

The Castel de Paolis vineyard, which is near Grottaferrata, has experimented with blending local wines with some other grapes and their white Vigna Adriana, which is excellent, uses Viognier. They also blend Syrah and Bordeaux grapes to create the good red Quattro Mori which moves very quickly off the enoteca shelves when it appears. At a more modest price, Casale del Giglio has some good bottles of white and red, and Paola di Mauro, of the di Mauro wine family, produces the Colle Picchioni wines that you can sample at her son's Roman restaurant, Il Sanpietrino, in piazza Costagutti near the Ghetto in the historic heart of Rome.

Porchetta alla Romana

Roman-style roast pork with herbs and wine

Romans are very fond of *porchetta* (meat from milk-fed baby pigs that weigh a minimum ten kilos), filled with fresh herbs, garlic, and spices, and basted with wine while roasting. The same effect can be achieved at home by using a boned leg of pork or, more economically, by using rolled belly of pork.

SERVES 6
PREPARATION TIME: 30 MINUTES
COOKING TIME: 25 MINUTES PER POUND OF MEAT (50 MINUTES PER KILOGRAM OF MEAT), PLUS AN EXTRA 20 MINUTES. PLUS 10 MINUTES RESTING TIME OUTSIDE THE OVEN AT THE END

2tbsp chopped fresh wild fennel
1tbsp chopped fresh rosemary needles
4 fresh sage leaves, chopped
1tsp ground nutmeg
4 garlic cloves, finely chopped
4tbsp extra virgin olive oil
1.8kg/4lb boned leg of pork
salt and freshly ground black pepper
250ml/9fl oz/scant 1¼ cups dry white wine

Preheat the oven to 150°C/300°F/ gas mark 2. Mix the fennel, rosemary, sage, nutmeg, and garlic with 1 tablespoon of the oil to make a thick paste. Season the pork with salt and pepper and spread the herb mixture over the inside. Roll up the meat tightly and tie in place with kitchen string. Brush the outside with a little more of the olive oil.

Put the meat in a roasting pan, pour on the remaining oil and the wine, and roast for 25 minutes per pound of meat plus an extra 20 minutes (50 minutes per kilogram of meat plus an extra 20 minutes) until the juices run clear when the thickest part of the meat is pierced with a skewer. Baste with the oil and wine while the meat is cooking.

Lift the meat from the pan and leave to rest in a warm place for 10–15 minutes before carving.

Pasta alla Checa

Summer tomato pasta with mozzarella and basil

This is a dish to make when the tomatoes are firm, ripe, and really fragrant. The quality of the tomatoes makes all the difference, so don't try it with anything but the best.

SERVES 4
PREPARATION TIME: 10 MINUTES, PLUS 30 MINUTES MARINATING
COOKING TIME: 10 MINUTES

500g/1lb 2oz ripe tomatoes
small handful of fresh basil leaves
salt and freshly ground black pepper
4tbsp extra virgin olive oil
200g/7oz mozzarella cheese, diced
500g/1lb 2oz spaghetti

Chop the tomatoes into quarters and tear up the basil leaves, leaving a sprig or two intact for garnishing. Combine the tomatoes and basil, season with salt and pepper, and add 2 tablespoons of the olive oil. Leave for 30 minutes, then stir in the mozzarella.

Bring a large pan of lightly salted water to the boil. Add the pasta and cook it according to the instructions on the pack until al dente. Drain the pasta, then, working very quickly, add the pasta to the tomato mixture and toss well. Pour in the remaining olive oil, toss again, and serve immediately.

L'Archeologia

L'Archeologia is on via Appia to the south of Rome, and used to be an old posthouse. In the winter months you can eat specialties from every part of Lazio, toasting yourself by an open fire, and in summer there are still regional Lazio specialties but the open fire gives way to the garden as the preferred place to sit while sipping a glass of white wine and eating a fish dish, such as acqua pazza (cooked in water flavored with chiles and tomato). You could start with a primo piatto pasta dish of spaghetti alla pescatora, which is with a sauce of seafood and fresh tomatoes. Secondi piatti include rabbit cooked with chile, garlic, rosemary, wine, and vinegar, or chicken with tomatoes and bell peppers cooked in wine. The unusually named cicoria pazza (which means crazy endive) is a side dish of boiled endive cooked with garlic, oil, and chile.

VIA APPIA ANTICA 139, 06 788 0494

Benito al Bosco

The bosco in the name of this restaurant refers to the wood of chestnut and pine trees that surrounds the outside dining area. This is a great summer escape from the capital, and Romans come here when the city holds its breath and the heat is almost an assault. There are good pasta dishes and the fish is always very fresh.

VIA MORICE 96, VELLETRI, 06 964 1414

La Briciola

Lighter versions of traditional dishes and interesting innovations provide good reasons for visiting this small restaurant. There are some fish dishes on the menu, but I come here for the good pasta and vegetables and the meat dishes. To finish, there is a small choice of delicious desserts.

VIA D'ANNUNZIO 12, GROTTAFERRATA, 06 945 9338

Cacciani

When Rome is sizzling, enjoy this ristorante's cool terrace with spectacular views. The restaurant was started by Nonno Leopoldo in 1922 and it has always served traditional dishes, such as pollo alla romana, and pasta cacio e pepe, and now the younger generation of the family is continuing the tradition. However, they have introduced some lighter innovations. The wine is from the family's own vineyard and the vegetables are either from Cacciani's kitchen garden or from small local producers.

VIA A. DIAZ 13/15, FRASCATI, 06 942 0378

Casale degli Archi

This is a family-run *agriturismo* (a type of farm-style trattoria), where they serve excellent dishes using their own produce, including simple meat and delicious vegetable and pasta dishes. I particularly enjoy the ravioli filled with home-grown vegetables and a pesto sauce made with arugula (rocket). On Sundays there is a delicious vegetable lasagne.
VIA APPIA KM23.400, 06 930 20893

Cecilia Metella

The same two brothers have been welcoming their guests here for many, many years. It is difficult to choose between the pasta baked in a crenellated dish (scrigno) and the wicked zite (large tubular pasta) alla prosciutto. Other pasta choices include fettucine with funghi porcini, and to follow, try roast gilthead, baked veal with potatoes, or turbot with olives.
VIA APPIA ANTICA 125/127,
06 511 0213

La Mia Goia

This is an interesting restaurant, because although the menu has all the great Roman dishes, including some *quinto quarto* (variety meats and offcuts) suggestions, they are usually adapted to make them lighter or an extra ingredient gives a new twist, such as the cacio e pepe with arugula (rocket). There is a list of Lazio wines or you can order a carafe of the owner's wine. Yet another attraction is that the prices are reasonable.
VIA RONCONI 9, GENZANO, 06 939 6143

L'Oste della Bon'Ora

This restaurant is in young hands with Massimo and Maria Luisa, but they are passionate about local food and only serve dishes made from top quality local produce. Starters include quails eggs with a truffle sauce, and primi piatti include ravioli with ricotta, spinach, and endive. If you have room for dessert, they serve delicious crêpes with a chestnut sauce.
VIA VENETO 133, GROTTAFERRATA,
06 941 3778

Ristorante Bucci

Bucci, in the historic center of Castel Gandolfo, is a family-run restaurant with a beautiful terrace looking out over Lake Albano. The traditional food, served in generous portions, includes several pasta dishes, porchetta, and home-made desserts.
VIA DE ZECCHINI 31,
CASTEL GANDOLFO, 06 932 3334

Taverna dello Spuntino

I have been coming to this delightful trattoria for years. It has a great atmosphere, with vegetables hanging from the beams and huge bowls of fruit on top of old cupboards. The Fortini family chooses first class produce and there is a great wine cellar that you can visit.
VIA CICERONE 22, GROTTAFERRATA,
06 945 9366

La Foresta

This large restaurant used to be known as "the king of the funghi porcini" and they are still one of its great specialties. The fettuccine with funghi porcini (ceps) is seriously good, and the portions are generous. There is a large tree-filled garden for outside dining, hence the restaurant's name. The only disadvantage of so much space is that it lends itself to wedding parties, so private diners try to avoid those days.
VIA DEI LAGHI KM12, ROCCA
DI PAPA, 06 9474 9167

Pages 190–1: Villa Aldobrandini is the grandest of the villas in Frascati and dominates the town. From its terraces there are beautiful views back to Rome.

189

Pannacotta con Frutti del Bosco

Molded "cooked" cream with a fruits of the forest (mixed berry) sauce

Pannacotta originated in Piemonte, but now that fresh cream is readily available, Roman restaurants have adopted it. It is often served with redcurrants, blackcurrants, wild strawberries, raspberries, or mixed berries.

SERVES 4

PREPARATION TIME: 20 MINUTES, PLUS 4 HOURS SETTING TIME

COOKING TIME: 2–3 MINUTES

2 leaves of gelatin or 1tsp granulated gelatin	BERRY SAUCE:
300ml/10fl oz/1¼ cups cream	250g/9oz/2 cups redcurrants, blackcurrants, wild
50g/2oz/¼ cup granulated sugar	strawberries, raspberries, or mixed berries
grated zest of 1 lemon	1tbsp superfine (caster) sugar
mint leaves for decoration	

Soak the leaf gelatin in cold water for about 10 minutes, until softened, then squeeze out the water. If using granulated gelatin, mix with 1 tablespoon water and let soften (bloom) for 5 minutes.

Put the cream, granulated sugar, and lemon zest into a small pan and bring to the boil. Simmer for 1 minute. Stir in the gelatin and pour into 4 custard cups (dariole molds). Leave the cups to cool to room temperature before placing them in the fridge for 4 hours to set.

Reserve a few berries for decoration. Purée the remaining berries with the superfine sugar. Pour through a sieve to remove any seeds.

Just before serving, turn out the creams and pour the berry sauce around the base of each one. Garnish with the reserved berries and the mint leaves.

Pasta con Funghi Porcini

Pasta with porcini mushrooms (ceps)

In Rome, some people prefer to use spaghetti with this recipe and others an egg pasta such as fettucine. It tastes good with either. Egg pasta might need more liquid, so it is a good idea to save 2–3 tablespoons of the pasta cooking water to add to the sauce.

SERVES 4

PREPARATION TIME: 10 MINUTES

COOKING TIME: 15 MINUTES

500g/1lb 2oz spaghetti or egg pasta such as fettucine	2 garlic cloves, finely chopped
3tbsp extra virgin olive oil	1tbsp fresh flat-leaf parsley, chopped
400g/14oz porcini mushrooms (ceps), scraped and sponged clean, if necessary, then sliced	salt

Bring a large saucepan of lightly salted water to the boil. Add the pasta and stir once until it is all submerged. Cook the pasta according to the instructions on the pack until al dente.

Meanwhile, heat the oil in a large skillet and cook the mushrooms and garlic over a low heat for 10 minutes, stirring frequently. Remove from the heat and stir in the parsley. Keep to one side until just before the pasta is ready and then return the pan to the heat.

When the pasta is cooked, drain, reserving 2–3 tablespoons of the cooking water if using egg pasta.

Toss the pasta with the mushrooms, adding some or all of the reserved water, if necessary, to moisten. Serve at once.

Acqua Roma

Although the old Italian proverb jokes *Acqua e pane, vita da cane* — "Bread and water, it's a dog's life", these are the first things to be brought to the table in any Roman trattoria. If Omar Khayyám had been Italian he would have proposed a loaf of bread, a jug of wine, and a liter of water! In ancient Rome the wine was always "cut" with water and today a wine glass and a water glass are always set on the table. Fashion conscious Italians do not walk round the city with a bottle of water, rather tradition permits them to bend down to drink from their beloved fountains, known as *nasone*.

I had been living in Rome for many years before I discovered that the drinking fountains and the beautiful ornamental fountains that you see all over the city enjoyed an intimate relationship with the old Roman aqueducts. The first aqueduct to bring water to the city was built in 312 BC, but by the time of the civil war and the assassination of Julius Caesar, Rome's water system had broken down. When Emperor Augustus came to power he set out to rebuild public morale, and in later life he boasted that he had transformed the republican city of brick into one of marble. All four existing aqueducts were old and leaking, so he asked his childhood friend Marcus Agrippa to develop the water system.

Marcus Agrippa ordered the construction of Aqua Julia (each aqueduct and its waters are named "Aqua"), and in the same year he built five hundred fountains and seven hundred basins and pools. In AD 13 work started on the construction of a complex of Roman baths behind the Pantheon, and Marcus Agrippa then built Aqua Virgo to bring the water to these baths.

The Roman Empire went into decline and when, in the sixth century AD, the barbarian invaders cut the aqueducts (and therefore the supply of water to Rome), the city fell. Aqua Virgo and Aqua Traiano continued to bring water to the city but they needed constant repairs, and as Rome began to grow under papal rule, it became clear that the city's water supply was inadequate. In the following years, many Popes brought drinking water to Rome by repairing and adapting the ancient aqueducts, and by building the beautiful fountains that Romans still enjoy today.

Aqua Vergine Antica and Aqua Vergine Nuova come from a small village near Tivoli, with both using the same spring formed by rainwater from the Alban hills. The water from the Antica flows by gravity, using the stone channels built by Marcus Agrippa, while the Nuova is pumped electrically before flowing in cast-iron pipes to supply domestic water to the city. Aqua Vergine Antica feeds the fountains in piazza del Popolo, piazza di Spagna, the Fontana delle Tartarughe (the tortoise fountain) in piazza Mattei, and the spectacular Fontana di Trevi. The water takes a day to get here and eighty thousand liters are needed each day. This water was often called "Trevi water", and English visitors used to claim that it was the only water to use to make a good cup of tea.

Pope Sixtus V repaired the old Aqua Alexandrina and renamed it Aqua Felice, after his own birth name of Felice. He is supposed to have been disappointed in the quality of the drinking water, complaining that it had no taste. Pope Paul V decided to bring water to the right bank of the River Tiber, because the residents of Trastevere had no adequate water supply. He repaired the old Aqua Traiana, which had been built by Emperor Trajan and brought in water from springs near Lake Bracciano. Today, Aqua Peschiers, which comes from fifty miles northeast of Rome, and Aqua Pia Marcia, which travels forty miles to the city, are considered to be the best quality waters. As you walk around Rome today you will see Romans drinking from the quaint street fountains. They are very proud of this tap water and will happily drink it in the street, but will always order bottled *acqua minerale* when they eat out.

Landmarks

As you leave Rome for the Albine hill towns, the largest gate in the Aurelian wall, Porta San Sebastiano, leads to the old Appian Way, via Appia Antica, which connects the capital to the port at Brindisi in Puglia in the "heel" of Italy. On either side of via Appia there are catacombs and thousands of ruined family tombs because under ancient Roman law no one could be buried inside the city walls for fear of disease.

Albano and Castel Gandolfo

Albano was easily reached from Rome by via Appia and Emperor Domitian built a huge villa here, with foundations stretching under the Pope's palace in Castel Gandolfo. The ruins of Domitian's fifteen-thousand seat amphitheater can still be seen, and the large cistern, which can store ten thousand cubic meters of water, is still used. The Church of Santa Maria della Rotonda was built on Roman ruins, and the remains of Caracalla's bath complex, built for the Roman legions garrisoned here is also visible. In 1944, heavy bombing revealed the town's original gate.

Albano almost joins the town of Castel Gandolfo. Both towns are built overlooking the lake (below) formed by the crater of an extinct volcano. The Palazzo Pontificio is the Pope's summer palace and there are different papal arms to be seen throughout the town. Palazzo Barberini is also Vatican property and the Barberini family emblem, bees, appears on many buildings. In 1929, Mussolini granted extraterritorial rights to the Vatican property in Castel Gandolfo, so there are Swiss Guards here, as well as in the Vatican. The observatory, built in 1936, dominates the hill, but conservation orders have ensured that the slopes on the southern shore are still covered

with chestnut and pine trees. The two roads linking the towns are called Galleria because the trees meet overhead. Traffic has ruined the lower road but the Galleria di Sopra still provides a pleasant walk with attractive views.

Ariccia

In 1854 a bridge was built over the ravine linking Ariccia (right) to Albano, so unfortunately there is now an increased amount of traffic in this lovely little town. In 1661 Alexander VII, the Chigi Pope, bought the town from the Savelli family and had Bernini redesign it. He added two side galleries to Santa Maria dell'Annunciazione and built a small sanctuary, Santa Maria di Galloro. Palazzo Chigi has a lovely facade and the Chigi family lived here until 1988, when it became the property of the town council. It is open to the public and well worth a visit.

Frascati

Frascati was badly bombed after the Anzio landing during World War II as the Germans fortified the Castelli to delay Rome being taken by the Allies. Many of the beautiful villas built in the seventeenth and eighteenth centuries by important Roman families were destroyed. The imposing Villa Aldobrandini is still intact, but the various fountains in the park, some of which portray great monsters, no longer work. The cascades of water were built to imitate the sound of the musical instruments being played by the statues. The villa is private but the park is open to the public. There is an octagonal Renaissance oratory next to the town hall and pieces of Roman temples were incorporated into the medieval church of Sant' Antonio. Piazza Marconi has a panoramic terrace from where you can marvel at the outstanding view. The Frascati area is known worldwide for the quality of its wine, and you pass serene vineyards (below) as you drive through.

Genzano

Genzano overlooks Lake Nemi, another extinct volcano crater, and in 1564 the village was acquired by the Sforza Cesarini family. The center has a round piazza where three streets meet before leading to Santa Maria della Cima, the church of the Capuchins, and the Sforza Cesarini Palace. In the center of the piazza a tall column, decorated with carved vine leaves, stands in the Fontana del Vino, which does in fact spout wine when the new wine is made. The palace was rebuilt by Gaetano Sforza Cesarini in 1713. The architect employed a trompe l'oeil technique to make the facade seem taller and longer.

The Olmate is an alley lined with elm trees that escaped the Dutch elm disease which destroyed so many elms in Europe in the late 1960s and 1970s, although wood from many of the trees was used for fuel during the war. Genzano is well known in the region for its wonderful bread.

Grottaferrata

The town grew up around the San Nilo Abbey, founded in 1004 by a Calabrian monk who followed the Greek rites. There had been so many Saracen attacks in the south that his brothers had become dispersed and he wanted to establish a new center. The abbey was built on the site of a Roman villa believed to have belonged to Cicero. The monks used stones from the ruined Roman villa and took twenty years to finish the work. It was consecrated in 1024 by Pope John XIX, before the division of the Church of Rome from that of Constantinople. Today the monks still follow the Byzantine order but they are under Papal protection. There is an interesting museum, a fine library of historic manuscripts, and a specialized center for repairing rare books and manuscripts.

Nemi

This is the smallest and perhaps the most attractive of the Albine hill towns (left). It was sacred to the goddess Diana, and her ruined temple stands on the slopes from the lake, which was known as lo specchio di Diana, Diana's looking glass. Caligula had large boats built for games and ceremonies on the lake, and although they were sunk, the soft mud kept them perfectly preserved. They were excavated in the 1930s and exhibited in a special museum. Unfortunately, they were burned by retreating German soldiers and the museum now houses only models. Palazzo Ruspoli, started in the fifteenth century, stands high above the lake. It has a Renaissance-designed facade which was remodeled in the eighteenth century, and a circular medieval tower which was built by the Orsini family.

Rocca di Papa

Situated at the top of a steep hill, Rocca di Papa (right) has always provided the strongest fortress in the Campagna region. In 1426 it belonged to the Colonna family, the Borgias bought it in 1501, and then it passed back into the hands of the Colonnas, until in 1816 it became the property of the Papal States. Hannibal is said to have camped here before attacking Rome.

Velletri

Velletri grew up on the site of an Etruscan settlement and was well developed in Roman times. Many patrician families built villas here during the days of the empire and Emperor Augustus spent his youth here. In the town museum there are many important exhibits, including a sarcophagus with reliefs depicting the labors of Hercules. Many buildings were destroyed by bombing in 1943, but one that is still standing is Santa Maria in Trivio, with a belltower erected in 1348. This was built to offer thanks for the abatement of the plague which afflicted the town that year.

Pages 200–1: the houses in the town of Rocca di Papa are stacked close together on the side of a steep hill. You are rewarded with superb views of the surrounding countryside after climbing to the top.

Glossary

Al dente: When applied to pasta, it means cooking until the pasta still feels firm when bitten into, but is not raw in the center.

Alimentari: Also sometimes called a drogheria, a general grocery store selling dry and packaged foods, and sometimes also cheeses and salami.

Aperitivo: Aperitif, a pre-dinner drink.

Caciotta: A semi-soft cheese.

Carciofi alla giudia: Whole artichokes with just the outer leaves and the inner hairy choke removed, then deep-fried in olive until crisp and golden. A dish that was introduced to Rome by the Jews.

Consorzio: An organization that controls the production standards of products governed by regulations.

Cucina povera: The tradition of using inexpensive and readily available regional produce to make dishes which are filling but cheap to make — in Rome cacio e pepe is an example of this.

Cupola: A domed roof.

Enoteca: Wine shop.

Exedra: In ancient Rome, a recess with raised seating.

Farro: Spelt, an old variety of wheat that was used by the Romans for making bread and pasta. It is now regaining popularity and is grown in Lazio, Umbria, and Tuscany.

Frappe: Fried puff pastry cakes.

Fresco: A painting made directly onto damp plaster so that the image becomes permanent.

Friggitore: Shop selling fried food such as deep-fried pumpkin flowers.

Gastronomia: Good quality grocery store.

Gelateria: An ice cream parlor.

Guanciale: A tasty specialty from Lazio made from pork cheeks cured in salt then air-dried for a few months. Pancetta (or, failing that, bacon) can be substituted but it does not have as much flavor.

Latteria: A dairy or store that sells milk, cream, butter, and cheeses.

Macelleria: Butcher's shop.

Magro: Days when according to the Cathoilc religion, you should not eat meat.

Melanzane alla parmigiana: Fried eggplant (aubergine) slices baked in a tomato sauce with mozzarella.

Norcineria: Traditional pork butcher's shop named after the town of Norcia in Umbria.

Osteria: The cheapest and simplest place to eat.

Panetteria: Bread shop.

Pangiallo: A fat-free cake made of dried fruit, almonds and hazelnuts.

Pasta cacio e pepe: Pasta with Pecorino cheese and black pepper.

Pasta e ceci: Pasta with garbanzo beans (chickpeas).

Pasticceria: A shop selling cakes, pastries, and cookies.

Pecorino: A hard cheese similar to Parmesan but made from sheep's milk rather than cow's milk. Pecorino romano is the best quality.

Pescheria: A fishmonger.

Pizza a taglio: A shop that sells pizza by the slice, wrapped in paper to take out.

Pizza bianca: Pizza dough with a simple topping, sometimes no more than olive oil and perhaps herbs.

Pizza rustica: Pizza bought by the slice to take out.

Polpette: Balls of meat or fish.

Prosciutto: Ham. Prosciutto cotto is ham that has been cooked, whereas the more commonly seen prosciutto crudo is raw ham. Parma ham and San Daniele are the two best quality examples.

Quartiere: District or neighborhood of a city.

Quinto quarto: Variety meats and offcuts.

Salame: Plural of salami.

Salumeria: A shop selling salami, mortadella, and cured meats such as prosciutto.

Taglioni: A pasta similar to tagliatelle, but narrower.

Tavola calda: A small establishment similar to a cafeteria that sells cheap and cheerful food such as salads, cold cuts, chicken roasted on a spit, and sandwiches, and sometimes soft drinks and perhaps beer. Food is ordered and paid for at the counter and then taken to a table.

Tonnarelli: A long pasta that resembles square spaghetti.

Trattoria: Between an osteria and restaurant in price and style. The food and service are generally family-style, and the dishes tend to be local.

Trompe l'oeil: Style of painting that appears to show a room or landscape by the use of perspective.

Variety meats: Offal.

Vicoletti: Small alleys.

Villa: In Renaissance architecture, a country residence. Sometimes used to describe the surrounding parkland.

Index